The Wooing of Beppo Tate

D1522226

Authors of the Caribbean

The Wooing of Beppo Tate

C. Everard Palmer

Nelson Thornes

First published in 1972 by:
André Deutsch Ltd

This edition published in 1979 by:
Nelson Thornes Ltd
Delta Place
27 Bath Road
CHELTENHAM
GL53 7TH
United Kingdom

13 / 40 39 38

A catalogue record for this book is available from the British Library

ISBN 978 0 17 566282 1

Printed by Multivista Global Ltd

This book is for
'Miguel' Paul and
John Palmer and Maureen Dunbar

Contents

CHAPTER I

A home at last

I was adopted and arrived in the night.

It's funny to begin with my first breakfast but it is appropriate as you will see. It alone told me much about what my new life would be like, this breakfast. It promised a life of plenty.

The sight of it tickled me. A neatly-piled plate of yellow steaming pegs of roast breadfruit and a bowl of equally steaming ackee and codfish. Yet another held chopped callaloo. Coffee steamed in a pot, fragrant as coffee could ever be. All this was a banquet to me and never was a room more compatible with my nostrils. For the first time in my life I was understanding the real meaning of plenty in terms of food. For it was poverty which, under all circumstances means little food to eat, had made my parents gladly consent to the Old Man adopting me.

When I was not speaking to him directly I called my new father the Old Man, but not because he was old. He was not more than forty-five, perhaps only forty. With a man like him it was difficult to tell. But he was handsome, with hair streaked with grey and soft as cotton, his nose non-flat and his features generally clean. He was a bachelor.

In any case my first impressions were that he and I would have a swell go of making home together.

His home was spotlessly clean – just like the man. A zinc roof over us, papered walls around and a floor mirror-bright from its weekend waxing and cleaning. I understood that a woman came in on Saturdays to clean the floor. It was Sunday, and I had arrived only the preceding night, but I was picking up things fast.

'Beppo?'

'Yessir.'

I cleaned my hands on my shirt tail.

'Sit down, m'boy.'

I put a lot of action into sitting down because I was hungry and also anxious to attack this luxury breakfast. I sat opposite him around a table that could accommodate four. Between us steamed the fragrant food which I had helped him prepare.

After grace we began to eat.

'Good?'

'Very good, sir. Where did you learn to cook like this?'

'Taught myself. You like it here?'

'I do, sir. I do.'

'What do you think o' the place generally?'

'It's a great place, sir. The hills and all. The greenness everywhere. The trees. First time I've ever seen so many breadfruits and mangoes in one place.'

'Mango season begins soon too. Then you will like it even better.'

'Oh boy!' I said. 'I can hardly wait.'

'But,' said the Old Man, pausing to fill his mouth with a quarter peg of breadfruit and some yellow ackee liberally mixed with codfish, 'be careful.'

'Of what, sir?'

'Don't be too impressed too fast. Things aren't always what they seem.'

'Oh?'

All the time I was busy eating. My Old Man wasn't quite as busy as I.

'The people . . . Some will be friendly and others . . .' He rocked his head. 'Most likely they'll deceive you.'

'Are there many boys?' I asked.

'More than enough.'

'I love to play with boys my age.'

'Nothing to fear from them boys,' the Old Man said. 'But there's a certain woman here I must tell you about.'

'Woman, sir?'

I didn't think I needed to be warned of a woman. She wouldn't bother me nor I her. It was the possibility of a bully being around that a boy had to fear. But the Old Man seemed serious enough.

'This woman . . .'

A knock on the door interrupted him and when I jumped up, ready to answer it, he motioned me to sit down. Apparently he knew who it was. Maybe the person's identity lay in the knock, perhaps he was expected.

'Come in,' called the Old Man.

And in he came, limping.

'Grab a chair, Teppy,' said the Old Man warmly.

Teppy carried his cap in his hand. The rest of his clothes were a khaki shirt and black pants. Perhaps his heavy moustache was worn to compensate for his baldness. His mouth, at first glance, seemed quite enormous. He appeared to be middle-aged. I guessed he was called Teppy because of his limping way to walk. Maybe the name was a corruption of Steppy. I didn't know for sure but was willing to bet a few pence that it could be so.

'This the young fella, Tate?'

'What d'you think of him?'

'Well . . .' He looked me over. 'Seems to me you picked the right one, Tate.'

'Sit down,' the Old Man said.

Teppy parked his cap on the back of his chair and sat.

The Old man produced another plate and knife and fork and a cup.

'Help yourself, Teps.'

'Oh goody,' said Teppy, making no bones about helping himself. For a time I was afraid he would help himself to everything and so I accelerated my rate of eating. 'Nothin' I like more'n a heavy Sunday breakfus',' he said. 'Lordy, Tate, the breadfruit look waxy like you butter 'em.'

'They're not buttered, Teps. They're cassava bread, that's why. They're the best,' said the Old Man, apparently meaning the variety of breadfruit which, as Teppy had said, was excellent. I myself had never before eaten roast breadfruit so waxy or so soft to the bite or so good tasting.

'What's your name, boy?' asked Teppy with a full mouth.

'Beppo.'

'Beppo?' A name which was no more uncommon than his own caused him to stop eating. 'Beppo?' He looked from me to the Old Man, who nodded. 'What's the worl's comin' to? People can't even fin' prop'r names for their fambly. 'Ow many o' you in your fambly, boy?'

'Ten,' I said.

'That explains it,' he said with a great show of wisdom. 'Your mammy and pappy done run out o' names.'

'Teppy isn't that fancy either, you know,' I said.

'What?'

The Old Man laughed boisterously. 'Good one, Beppo. Put him in his place.'

His compliment made me wax warm. 'How'd you get such a name, Teppy?'

His eyes shot up big and bright.

'I bet there's twenty in your family,' I said.

My Old Man laughed again.

Teppy said, 'This boy's too perky, Tate. He's too perky for me.'

'That's the kind o' boy I like. One to stand on his own. I was just aiming to tell him about my dear and beloved neighbour, when you came in.'

'Oh yes. He needs to know about that virago.'

'That who?' I asked.

'Virago, boy. Devil woman. You'll be 'earin' plenty o' Mrs Beltshazzar.'

'Belmont,' corrected the Old Man. 'Her name's Belmont.'

'Beltshazzar,' insisted Teppy. 'You'll soon bear me witness, boy, that I'm right.'

'Why not call him by his name, Teppy? I'm sure he'd appreciate it.'

'What's your name, boy?'

'Beppo, I told you.'

'Goodness, Tate. I'd rather 'e was called Nebuchadnezzar.'

I decided to let him win the name-calling game. He was the most dedicated eater I had ever seen, keeping his head almost always down over the plate, scooping up the food as fast as possible. Even his moustache was eating. He didn't have great confidence in chewing at all and swallowed after the second attempt at that necessary action.

'Who is Mrs Beltshazzar anyway?' I asked, all the while eating as fast as I could, hoping to keep up with Teppy.

'Mrs Belmont,' said the Old Man. 'I don't want you to be copying Teppy's ways. He's okay in certain respects, Beppo, and he'll be here most Sunday mornings, bright and early for breakfast, but he's not the best o' company.'

'Lordy, Tate, what's this you tellin' the boy?'

'Her name's Belmont,' the Old Man said to me. 'Not that infernal Beltshazzar.'

'You know,' said Teppy, taking time to clean his teeth

with a massive pink tongue. 'You know, every time you talk 'bout that Mrs Beltshazzar, I get to thinkin' that you really don't hate the woman at all, Tate . . .'

'What?' shot the Old Man, freezing.

'It's true, Tate. You's always takin' up for 'er.'

'Taking up? For her? Me?'

'Oh yes. You's always callin' 'er name pretty like.'

He laughed loudly, his teeth reminding me of the ruins of Stonehenge.

'Look here, Teppy . . .'

But he ignored the Old Man. 'You lissen 'ere, boy. Mrs Beltshazzar's one to watch. She's likely to blaze up any time at you. No matter 'ow you need to adventure never adventure yourself on 'er lan' 'cause if she doesn' give you a soun' t'rashin' right on the spot she might 'ave you in court. She's likely got traps set on 'er lan' for you to fall in anyway . . .'

'Traps?'

'Yes, traps. Boy traps. If you ever see the bes' mango in your life over at 'er place never set foot there to get that mango 'cause that'll be it.'

'You're frightening the boy, Teppy.'

'Fright'nin' 'im, Tate?' he said. 'God forbids. I'm lettin' 'im know where 'e stan' wit' the lady. Look, boy, if you see 'er little gal givin' you the once-over, you look the other way.'

'She's got a girl?' I asked.

'Oh yes,' said the Old Man. 'Mrs Belmont lost her husband some years ago. Two years, Teppy? Three?'

'T'ree, Tate, an' you ought to know better'n me. But you watch that gal, boy,' continued Teppy. 'She's likely to get you into all kinds o' pitfalls. She'll cuddle up to you an' . . .'

'Cuddle? Are you crazy? I don't like girls.'

Teppy looked at the Old Man. 'Aren't they all the same,

Tate? They don't like gals, they don't like gals. Nex' thing you know they're followin' gals aroun' everywhere.'

'Not me.'

'You're frightening Beppo, Teppy.'

'The boy's t'be prop'ly briefed, Tate. If you won't do it I will. Where you from, boy?'

'St Elizabeth.'

'That's a mighty big place, boy. Where exac'ly?'

'Santa Cruz.'

'Aunha. I know it. Passed t'rough umpteen times. Had a lady frien' there, too.'

My Old Man looked at me and screwed up his mouth. He said, 'You going to church today, Teppy?'

'Of course I goin' t'church. I got to give the good Lord thanks for sparin' me life an' providin' for me.'

I realized then that a bell had begun to ring.

'That's the first bell,' said the Old Man, reading my thoughts.

'How many bells will ring then, sir?'

'Three.'

'Are we going?'

Teppy said, 'Of course you's goin'. Tate an' me never miss a Sunday.'

When the Old Man challenged this statement with a hard look, Teppy added, 'Barrin' sickness an' bad weather an' such things, we never miss.'

The Old Man got up. I did likewise, helping him to clear the table of dishes.

'We have work, Teppy.'

'So you 'ave.'

'Beppo and I are working men.'

I rather liked to be called a man although I was only nearing eleven.

'You's bent on insultin' me, Tate. As if I don' work.'

'Oh you do, you do,' said the Old Man.

'Does he?' I asked.

'Now, look what you done,' complained Teppy. 'Give your boy wrong ideas 'bout me. An' so blinkin' soon!'

I liked Teppy. He seemed an out-and-out joker. I judged him as a happy-go-lucky bachelor, capable of talking himself into obtaining anything of anybody. As the Old Man had said, he ate many of his Sunday breakfasts with him. I wondered where he ate Sunday dinner. He was a lovable rascal.

'See you in church,' said the Old Man.

Teppy looked at me. 'Tha's 'is way o' gettin' rid o' me, boy. 'E an' I be frien's a long time but 'e never fails to insult me each time 'e wan's me to go. See you in church 'e says an' 'e really means for me to get lost. All right. 'Ere I go.' He lit his pipe, rose and took his cap. 'See you in church then,' he said and began to limp out. Lovable Teppy.

At the door he paused and said to me, 'Be good to Tate, boy. 'E's the bes' man in this whole village. Many a woman'd give 'er littl' finger to marry 'im. 'E's the bes'.'

And he was gone.

The Old Man chuckled and shook his head.

But I agreed with Teppy. I didn't know yet if my foster father was the best man or not in the village nor did I know if the women found him attractive, but this much I did know. He was kind. Already he had changed my life radically. I had been catapulted from poverty into comfort. Usually children who, like me, were taken from their parents didn't fare so well. The prime motive was to secure them as mini-workhorses, a boy or girl, who would do tasks around the house and farm, the menial the more fitting. But I could already see that my luck was excellent, that I had fallen into a feathered bed.

Somehow I was happy that the Old Man was not married. Sometimes it was the woman who made life miserable for people like me. And if he had been married he'd most likely have a child or two of his own, children who'd come first and I'd be a mere addition, and from the bottom up at that.

But this was living.

He had already bought new clothes to replace my rags and I was given a room all my own, a decorated room, clean, comfortable and with papered walls. At my former home I had shared one, sardine-packed with four of my brothers.

My bed was real too, carpenter-made but with a real mattress which was filled with soft bed grass raked from the hills. At home we children slept on rags which we spread on the floor each night.

But everything was different now.

While the Old Man washed the dishes and I dried, I asked him why he and Mrs Belmont were enemies.

'Oh,' he said. 'It's not much of a reason. See that buggy outside?'

'Yes, sir. It's very nice. I love buggies.'

It was beautiful, too, a black box with red streamers and a grey canvas top.

'That buggy belonged to the Belmonts. A few months before he died Bill, that was his name, decided to sell. Of course I didn't know that the poor woman fought with Bill not to sell it. So I bought. Well, seems as if I bought more than the buggy, Beppo, because we've been feuding, Mrs Belmont and I, ever since. She thinks I took advantage of her. By just buying the buggy. When, if I hadn't, someone else would have. She hates me 'cause I bought it. I've offered to sell it back to her but there's nothing doing, Beppo. She won't buy and she won't talk. Silly woman . . .'

'Would you really sell it back to her, sir?'

'Of course I would, I told you. Anything for the sake of peace. I've offered it several times.'

'Oh no.'

I wished she wouldn't buy because I liked the buggy and wanted it to remain in our family. Buggies were next to cars.

I couldn't say that I relished the idea of the Old Man and his neighbour continuing this quarrel but if peace meant losing the buggy I wasn't for it at all. Let them feud.

From that moment on I desired so badly to meet Mrs Belmont, to see what kind of woman would keep a quarrel going for such silly reasons.

As if he read my thoughts the Old Man said, 'You'll probably meet her today, Beppo. Mrs Belmont's a regular churchgoer.'

'Yes, sir,' I said.

Two plus two

The Old Man and I went to church in style. I got my chance to ride in the buggy. The seats were padded and the carriage smelt of new paint. It was pulled by a black-and-white horse we called Boysie.

We jogged down the gravel road lined by mango and breadfruit, with the odd coconut tree teetering over. Sugar cane was everywhere and almost every plot of land had a farmhouse on it. As we slipped over a bridge I peered over the side into the pool below the slipway.

'Do you like to fish?' the Old Man asked.

'Yes, sir.'

'You do much fishing in your part o' the country?'

'No, sir.'

'You do any at all?'

'No, sir.'

'H'mm,' the Old Man said, understanding.

We passed people on the road, church-bound people like us, and the Old Man raised to them his whip in salute and they grinned back or spoke how-de-dos. Women and girls in pure white and frills and men in full suits of black or white or something else. They hadn't left their pipes at home, neither had the Old Man.

The Old Man never once used his whip on Boysie. I guessed he carried it along as a part of a buggy's trappings. And that horse didn't need whipping either. He pulled with the strength of an elephant, only faster and seemed to enjoy it immensely.

The road swung around a sharp turn and climbed a hill and Boysie slowed to a walk and pulled in earnest. The iron-banded wheels crunched stones.

I really liked the country, the trees and plants being everywhere, the lot buzzed by bees and birds and butterflies, the air sweetened by blossoms of one kind or another, and the hills squeezing in on everything. A few john crows wheeled in the cloud-patched sky.

Just as we got into the churchyard the third and last bell began to ring.

'Just in time,' the Old Man said.

'We start now?'

'Anytime now,' he said. 'Parson's not here yet.'

'How'd you know?' I asked.

' 'Cause I don't see his car, that's how, Beppo.'

Indeed there was no car in the yard, only our buggy and two others and an assortment of saddled mules and donkeys.

'Where's parson from, sir?'

'Lucea.'

'Where's that, sir?'

'Some sixteen miles away,' he told me.

'A long way.'

'Not by car,' he said.

He allowed me to hitch the horse and scatter in front of the animal the bundle of guinea grass which I had insisted we bring along.

A sprinkling of men was in the yard, in small groups, hands in their pockets or on their chins, conversing, laughing and greeting newcomers.

Teppy was there. Detaching himself from one of the groups, he came forward to greet us. He looked different, dressed as he was in a black suit and a broad but crushed neck tie. He almost looked smart.

'Hi there, Teppy,' the Old Man said.

'Hullo, hullo.'

A small black Bible and a maroon-coloured prayer book were in his hands.

'Boy,' he said to me, 'you better go inside an' get what's lef' o' the Sunday school.'

I looked to the Old Man for him to confirm the order. He said, 'Why go now? It's over now anyway, Teppy.'

'But in the footur,' said that gentleman, ''e should be 'ere.'

'I'll see he gets what he's to get, Teppy,' the Old Man said impatiently.

Notes from an organ floated out into the yard.

'You can't beat organ music,' said Teppy as he led us to the group from which he had just come. It was as though he thought the Old Man to be a stranger to these men.

'Gen'elmen,' said he. ''Ere's Tate an' 'is littl' boy. Say hullo, boy.'

'Gentlemen,' the Old Man said, 'meet Beppo.'

'Spunky fella,' said Teppy.

The Old Man eyed him but let it pass.

'The boy you been tryin' to get eh, Tate?' asked one man. He smelt of camphor balls and his hair was mercilessly brilliantined.

'Yep.'

'Oh!'

Walking around me as though I was an object for sale, they looked me over.

One wanted to know where I was from.

Teppy told him.

Another asked if my parents were dead.

Teppy said, 'Dead? No, sirs. They busy makin' chil'ren.'

The Old Man barked, 'Look here, Teppy. That's enough

of your confounded nonsense. I won't have you insult Beppo.'

'I like 'im, Tate,' said one man. 'I need a boy meself. How many boys in your family, boy?'

'My name's Beppo,' I said politely.

All the men exchanged glances.

Teppy said, 'Aunha. What'd I tell you? He's a spunky one all right.'

Everybody suddenly turned to something else.

Into the yard came a woman and a girl. They were wearing angel-white and the girl was covered in frills. If I knew my onions she was about my age. The woman had a bony yet very attractive face due mainly to her high cheek bones and clearly ridged nose. But hers was a serious face all right.

'Aunha,' said Teppy.

By the way everybody was reacting I knew that the woman and girl were important. Having passed them on the road, I had noticed that the Old Man had not waved his whip at them. At that time it had meant nothing but now it was significant. It must be Mrs Belmont and her daughter.

The girl was no less attractive than the mother and had what I thought, at a glance, to be an unforgettable face.

All the men watched them respectfully, occasionally throwing the Old Man a searching glance.

They passed very close to us, their backs arrow-straight, the girl throwing me a little something in the way of a girlish but hostile look. She knew who I was.

'Now you's paired off,' said Teppy. 'You an' the old woman, Tate. The boy an' the gal.'

'Who says?' barked the Old Man.

The men laughed. One said, 'Teppy's got a point, Tate. Did you see the look the little missy cast Beppo?'

'I saw nothing,' said the Old Man, snorting. He quickly modified the statement. 'I saw it but there's nothing in it.'

'And Mrs Belmont isn't old, Teppy,' I said.

'So you's takin' up for 'er too!' he said.

The Old Man was very irritable, a lot more than he ought to have been by the few comments that had been made. Yet with all his irritation, I noticed that he had not once taken his eyes off Mrs Belmont until her very back had disappeared in the arch-shaped church door. Then he began to breathe easily again.

Organ notes continued to filter through between bashes of the bell.

The man with the brilliantined hair said, 'I goin' to get parson to be peacemaker between you two, Tate.'

The group laughed.

'I can handle my own affairs, Ned,' said the Old Man.

They would have pulled his leg further but abruptly the bell ceased to ring. The road was smoking and somebody said, 'Parson's coming.'

We went towards the church.

The pews were nearly all taken and the general arrangement was, except for the very young who must be babysat by mothers, adults were at the back and children in the front.

It was a place for queer Sunday dresses and strange hats, old jackets, perfume and tobacco and bald heads. The Old Man motioned me to a front pew; he went to the rear.

The only vacant seat was beside Mrs Belmont's girl. I didn't know what to do at all. I didn't wish to be involved in their stupid quarrel. I wished there was another seat. I looked to the Old Man for help, pointing out the vacant seat. He understood my predicament but nodded. I sat.

The girl pulled away from me, squeezing the others to the right and, by this action, almost making room for another child. Our eyes met. She was a cool cucumber all right. I was sure we would clash and afraid she would win. Like mother, like daughter? Teppy might have been right. Were we paired off, me with her, the Old Man with her mother?

For the next few minutes we were engaged in looking over our noses at each other and gradually, without realizing it, she relaxed and the space between us dwindled though it never vanished.

The organist was busy pumping the organ, skating her fingers across the keyboard and pulling out and sinking stops. Behind her were three rows of pews semi-filled with women in white. The choir.

Then suddenly a voice said, 'Let us pray.'

I turned. The minister was at the end of the aisle. A tall dark man dressed in a black gown with a huge white cape thrown over his shoulders.

Everybody knelt.

Teppy seemed to be everything including a show-off. While the others contented themselves with kneeling like ordinary folk, he flung his head up and back, his hands clasped up and under his chin so that his closed eyes, were they open, would be regarding the ceiling. No doubt he intended himself to look the most religious man in the congregation, and most of us boys spent some of our prayer time looking back and stealing glances at him through half-closed eyes; although a good number of the brats shared their interest equally between me and Teppy, the saint.

On the faces of the boys I could read all sorts of questions concerning me.

Who is he?

Where did he come from?

I wonder if I can lick him.

'Hymn number . . . ,' said the minister and before he could even complete what he was saying everybody jumped off his knees and into standing position. For the next few seconds most people buzzed others to find out which number hymn the minister had called out. The organist played a chord, preparing us for the tune, and the congregation burst into the song with a right joyful noise.

Because I didn't know the hymn I considered it good sense to chew my mouth as though I were singing, but I wasn't saying a blessed thing. With the exception of *Jesus* and *Lord*, the words were Greek to me. Many of the other boys were doing the same as well, chewing the mouth I mean, but singing nothing. One who was acting tough by not even attempting to chew his mouth, was first elbowed in the head by a woman who seemed a grandmother, then when that failed the poor fool nearly had his ear clipped off by the sharp edge of her Hong Kong-made fan. While he held on to it, giving it succour, he quickly started one of the most authentic mouth-chewing singings I had ever witnessed. The fool.

But the men – they were lusty singers even though they were definitely off-key with different basses full of energy. Teppy? Oh boy! He was now wearing steel-rimmed glasses and was not only holding his hymn book at arm's length but also up, for all to see rather than for himself to see.

Ahead of the minister came a procession of surpliced boys. Where did they come from? They must have been in the vestry all the time. The head boy carried a symbolic metal cross while the last one, the one just in front of the minister, carried the collection plate.

I liked the whole thing immensely and took it in greedily, craning above the head of others to see. You see I had not been accustomed to attending this kind of church at all. When I was back at home I belonged to no church but used to drop in at some pocomania meetings. Pocomaniaism is a sort of religion practised in booths and at village squares, with cymbals and drum-beating and people claiming to

25

have got the spirit, but this was something I thought I'd like in a big way. The drums and cymbals of pocomaniaism were missing, and the general jumping-up of the converts too; but we had the organ here and the surplice boys. I wished I were a surplice boy. I would have to ask the Old Man if I might become one.

The girl beside me, Mrs Belmont's daughter, that is, eyed me with scorn and superiority, seemingly pitying me for my fascination with the rituals which she had grown so accustomed to. So, quickly, I adjusted my face to hide my deep interest in the procession though I watched it all the way, all the way to the altar where each boy bowed deeply then stepped left and joined the white-clad women in the choir. Oh boy!

As a matter of fact the entire service held me spellbound and whenever we sang, which was often, I chewed my mouth. Mrs Belmont's girl knew I was pretending to be singing and decided to show me up as the cheat I was. She waited until we were on the last hymn. Imagine that, the very last. She decided to share her hymnal with me but you'll soon see that it wasn't her good nature that motivated her. I held on to one side of the book but couldn't make head or tail of the song as, in her book, the notes of the music and the words of the hymn were written one line here, another below and so on. Very confusing. I couldn't follow.

When she noticed my confusion she smiled with so much of her superiority. I thought I was going to hate that girl.

'Can't read?' she said at last.

'I can too,' I almost shouted above the singing.

'Well, *sing*!'

'You can't make me!'

'Dunce!'

What kind of Christian was she anyway? Yes, what kind was she? Throughout the service she had taken so much care not to let any part of her body touch mine as though she thought I was a leper. Now she had insulted me. At least, if she hated me because I was now the son of the Old Man whom she hated, she could have pretended to have some Christian principles while she was in church and waited to get at me outside. Or at school. Yes, school. We'd meet there and probably have some of the most glorious clashes.

When the service was over and the Old Man, as others were doing, was waiting in line at the door to shake hands with the minister and to commend him for the splendid sermon delivered, Teppy took me aside.

''Ow'd it go? 'Ow'd you make out, son?' In his Sunday charity he had switched from boy to son in addressing me.

'Make out?'

'Yes. 'Ow'd the firs' encounter go?'

'The service was fine. I liked it.'

'Not the service, son. You didn' 'ear a word o' what the goodly parson said. You was eyein' that Mrs Belmont's wench.'

Even Mrs Belmont had come in for some of his Sunday charity. He hadn't called her Beltshazzar.

'You been lookin' at 'er all the time,' he said.

'It's a lie.'

'I see the whole thing. You can't fool me. Nex' thing Tate knows you'll be over by 'er place helpin' 'er to chop wood an' . . .'

'Does she have to chop wood?'

'What you think? She lives in a bed o' roses?'

'Why does Mrs Belmont allow that?'

'You seen the woman, you seen 'er face. She's a mean one. Aunha, she is.'

The Old Man was joining us.

'Hi, Tate,' Teppy said with deception. 'What a fine

27

sermon parson preached to us, eh? Everyday 'e gets better'n better. ''E touch me t'day clear down in me toes, Tate. I was tremblin' mos' o' the time. I was jus' tellin' your new son that wit' a couple more o' parson's sermons 'e'll be turnin' the other cheek to 'is enemies.'

'Beppo has no enemies,' the Old Man said.

''E'll soon 'ave.'

'Why should a little boy have enemies, Teppy, you . . . !'

'For the same reason men 'ave,' he said.

Just then Mrs Belmont and the girl went by and again all conversation in our small group came to an unnatural suspension and I began to think that the Old Man might, after all, deep down and in true marrying spirit, like that woman.

Teppy removed his spectacles the better to wink at me as much as to say: 'I goin' to see you follow that girl aroun' to the ends o' the worl', boy.'

I didn't know about that.

We soon dispersed to go home and Teppy mounted his saddled donkey, a pitiful-looking animal that was mostly bones.

CHAPTER 3

Blackmail

While my Old Man cooked Sunday dinner of rice-and-peas and roast beef and gravy, I wandered on the farm, getting acquainted with the place in general and with the animals and the river that sliced through. I pulled deep lungsfull of country air into my system.

This farm, which he called the house farm, was about one-third of his holdings. He had another farm of sugar-cane elsewhere, some forty acres large, but this one was mixed, with bananas and yams and farm animals.

The part of the land which sloped up from the river was shared seventy, thirty by bananas and yams, but the flat stretch which was damper than the rest, was the pasture. It was dotted with thinned guava trees and the occasional bread fruit. It grazed six cows and calves altogether and Boysie, the horse. Five goats and some poultry made up the rest of the animal population.

The river looped through the land with various water plants and bamboo trees keeping it company. The bed was very rocky in parts but tracts of sand formed the concave sides of the loops. Rounded river stones of various colours and sizes were strewn along the course and the pools were everywhere. I looked forward to bathing in the best of them but since there was hardly any fun in doing this alone I thought I should wait until I had made me at least one friend.

Tall coconut trees, scattered on the farm, swayed gently.

At the same time that I browsed about I thought of Mrs Belmont's daughter. Already we had clashed – and in church – so I expected more of the same and quite worse, because our clashes would be of a more secular nature from then on. Yet I found myself thinking of her in a nice way – if you get what I mean – wishing that instead of being what she was, she would be kind, well-disposed to me and talking to and taking up for me in my troubles with others. If there were going to be troubles. After all we were neighbours and from where I walked now I could see her home, the roof anyway. What nonsense that the adults were quarrelling. We shouldn't have to do the same. I lived alone with the Old Man and she alone with her mum, what better thing than for us to live neighbourly?

Although I made no conscious effort I found that I remembered her face clearly: the clean profile and the ivory of her teeth and the baby-clean white of her bright burning eyes. There was a mole on her upper lip that helped to make her pretty, by george. And that pony tail of hers was cute. Ah, well, we would see what we would see. Tomorrow would be school and we would at least meet, if not in the same class, then during the recess period when all the school was one.

For some reason, as I walked along or leaned against the barbed wire fence, I began to think of Teppy. He didn't live far from us. I could see wisps of smoke. Maybe I should run up to his house, I thought, and saunter about and see if he wouldn't have more to say about those Belmonts. They intrigued me. And the more you know of an enemy the better you are able to fight him.

Hopping over the fence, I crossed the river teetering atop a single log that lay sprawled by some windstorm, and dashed through the banana trees up the grade and into his yard.

The place was desolate.

The lawn was overgrown with grass and runners and the fence had rotted in places. There was an outdoor building, the kitchen. The only worthy-looking thing in that entire yard turned out to be a large spreading mango tree. Its branches bore a heavy burden of dozens, maybe hundreds upon hundreds of green mangoes. To me they seemed like mangoes of distinction. I'd give them another week or two and they'd start ripening. I had better make friends with Teppy, so that I'd receive gifts of mangoes.

The walls of the house were in a bad state, too. Made of board, they had rotted in parts and been patched over with oil drums which had been cut open and pressed flat into sheets. The roof was of zinc sheets of different sizes, colours and shapes. The rust-coloured zinc were the old ones.

A vine-like plant swarmed up the verandah rails to the roof. If trimmed it would have enhanced the place but it was just as neglected as everything else.

I wondered what Teppy did with his time, why he had allowed his property to run down like this. What a difference it made with my Old Man's spick-and-span place.

Ah well . . .

I mounted the sagging steps to the verandah.

'Who's that?' he barked from inside the house. His mouth seemed full.

'Me,' I said.

'Who the ram goat is me?'

'Me, Beppo.'

'Oh you. What you want, boy?' Not very warm.

'Just visiting,' I said.

'Never 'ear of a boy visitin' a fifty-year-ol' man,' he said again with a full mouth, 'but come in.'

I walked in and was appalled.

He was eating all right but it was not that that appalled

me. He was eating from a single vessel, but what a vessel. It was what was called a pudding pan, about eight inches deep, made of tin and cylindrical in shape but widening at the top. It was the sort of thing most women took to the market on their heads and returned with full of this and that but mainly of slabs of beef and layers of fish. It wasn't an eating vessel but a carrying one and enormous. It must have been at least a cubic foot in volume, and it was just about full of food which was in a state of mush.

The house was stuffy and old and badly kept. The floor was sagging and dirty, with dust swept under the table which was rickety, and the paper of the walls had peeled in many places. A glass pane of one window had been replaced by cardboard. Rats could be heard scudding across the race track of the ceiling, kicking up their dung which had hardened to sound like gravel.

'You're eating,' I said by way of opening a conversation.

'An' so I is,' he said, eating with a fork which had seen many a dining. So battered was it that it had lost a prong and the handle was twisted out of shape.

Good manners demanded that he offer me something to eat though I was sure that my stomach was not strong enough to accept the kind of food he was eating. Anyway he held up a piece of meat on his fork and he said, 'Would you like a piece o' snake meat, boy?'

I made a face. 'Snake meat?'

'That's right, boy,' he said, setting the meat into his mouth and pulling it off the fork. He chewed it only twice before he swallowed it. As it slowed in his throat he made an effort to swallow harder and send it on its way down.

'It's good, boy, this snake meat. If you only want a piece let me know an' I'll be mighty glad to dish you up some.'

'Boy,' I said.

But he held up yet another piece of meat. 'Look at this fine piece o' alligator jowls,' he said. 'Care to try it?'

By this time I was ready to vomit. I had also figured his was a kind of diplomacy to discourage me from accepting any of his food. The rat, I thought, and to think that the Old Man had fed him so royally only that morning.

'No, Teppy,' I said, 'I don't want to try it. I'm not hungry.'

'Oh.' His face suddenly brightened. 'What brings you a-visitin'?'

'Nothing.'

'Now, that's an answer to beat all answers,' he said, crushing a hunk of yam with a single chewing motion and, balling it with his cow-like tongue, swallowed it. 'What brings you I ask an' you say nothin'. Now I'm not that bright, sholy, but if I go visitin' you can bet me gran'mother's necklace that I go visitin' for somethin'.'

'Well, I'm just looking around.'

He didn't answer me but continued to eat at an alarming pace. I said, 'Jeez, Teppy, you have a fine mango tree outside!'

'An' so I 'ave, boy. Start savin' your money 'cause I'll soon be 'avin' mangoes to sell you an' all the res'. They's the bes' mangoes this side o' the Atlantic Ocean. Save your money. A thro pence will buy you twelve.'

'Twelve for three pence! But that's expensive!'

'They're expensive mangoes,' he said. 'Is that why you come visitin'?'

'No. I told you. I'm only looking around. I hope you don't mind.'

'God forbids, boy. But I always think that boys fin' more int'restin' subjec's than ol' bachelors. Take that Beltshazzar wench . . .'

'Why do you call her wench?'

33

'You rather I call her gal?'

'No, no. What's wrong with girl?'

His rate of eating was hardly affected by our conversation.

'What's wrong wit' girl?' he asked. 'It's plum' jaw-breakin' sayin' girl, tha's what, when they's easier words such as gal an' wench.'

'Well, use her name,' I said, hoping he'd let out the secret of her name. 'You could say instead, Hilda. Or Esmeralda . . .'

'Hilda!' he shot. 'Esm'ralda! Why you think that poor littl' wench's called by mule names, boy?'

Why I had selected those names out of the blue I knew not. But Teppy went on: 'Why Hilda an' the confounded Esm'ralda an' not Daphne?'

'Is that her name?' I said, stepping forward. Daphne was a cute name.

'Huh!' he snapped as though I had said something offensive.

'Is her name Daphne?'

He burst out laughing, coughing on some snake meat or alligator jowls or perhaps lizard gizzards. 'So that's it!'

'That's what?' I asked, withering.

'That's what you come visitin' to fin' out! That wench's name! Well, I'll be doggone,' he said, cocking his head to one side then the other and even suspending his military operations in the pudding pan. 'You're a fast worker, boy. You beat me col'. When I was young an' in me prime an' bent on courtin', I couldn' 'a' work faster. Wait till I tell Tate 'bout your fas' foot works.'

'Tell Dad?'

'Why not?' he said, returning to his battle against the food.

'You wouldn't.'

'I aim to, boy.'

'But why? I didn't come for that, Teppy. Honest.'

'You tellin' a man 'is business, boy?'

'I came visiting. I told you.'

'Visitin' me backfoot! I know why you come all right.'

'Please don't tell,' I said.

'All right, boy. But 'ow much you willin' t'pay?'

'Pay?'

He was not the lovable rascal I had thought him to be. He was more like a robber.

'You catch fish?' he asked me.

'No.'

'Shoot birds?'

'No, sir.'

I was frightened out of my wits by the prospect that I was being prepared for some sort of blackmail.

'So you don't fish an' you don't shoot birds! Too bad,' he said, 'for it so 'appens that I like the taste o' crayfish, boy, an' every littl' boy 'ere if 'e be ever so littl', every boy 'as a catapult an' I can't see why not you. Unless, of course, you want me to tell Tate 'bout your spoonin'.'

'I'm not spooning,' I protested.

'But you aim to, eh? Now I'm not so sure that Tate will like to know that you's sidin' up to that Beltshazzar wench. I believe 'e'll feel betrayed an' undercut by you, boy. 'Ere 'e is kickin' up a fuss that Mrs Beltshazzar hates the daylights out o' 'im an' you comes along an' start t'be bosom frien's o' the dauter. 'E'll be furious all right. 'E'll be like the king o' bad eggs. Every jack man an' woman'll fault 'im for bein' the enemy. Poor Tate, they'll all say that 'e's the one respons-s'ble for keepin' the feud goin' all this time. I tell you, boy, 'e's likely to sen' you packin'. You like it 'ere, don't you?'

'Yes.'

'An you like Tate, too, eh?'

'Of course I do. You know that.'

'Well, don' let 'im sen' you away. You couldn' 'a' foun' a better man to take you in.'

'But I didn't come here to find out the girl's name.'

'Aunha. Aunha,' he said, nodding his head but not believing a word I was saying.

I guessed I was licked.

'What do you want?' I asked.

'Now you talkin' sense, Beppo or Leppo or whatever they call you. What I want? Two crayfish everý week. The giant ones like lobsters. We call 'em mountains. Two mark you. An' as for birds. 'Ow 'bout two per week, too? I like pigeons, baldpates an' lapwings bes'.'

'But . . .'

'I knows you don't own a fish pot, boy. But Tate'll 'ave one made for you. Go on home an' express an int'rest in the fishin' industry an' 'e'll get you one. Tate'll bend over backwards for you. I know the man. 'E loves you like I love crayfish an' bird's meat.'

'And you aim to capitalize on that, eh?'

'Boy, don' give me any o' that sassy talk now! Or else?'

I walked out of his stuffy old house and out on to the porch where the air was remarkably fresh and cool. I felt like a rag. Indeed worse than a rag. My interest in the girl had really got me in deep all right. Teppy had caught me. Why had I come? Why? I was trapped.

Two mountain crayfish per week and two birds. Rats. A catapult I could manage on my own but it meant that I would be forced to broach the subject of a fishpot to the Old Man and God knew I had no mind, as yet, to bother him with requests. It wasn't good policy. Not decent. He had taken me in and given me a good home and plenty to eat and was treating me as he would his own son. He called me son and I styled him Dad, when speaking to him. What better could a boy expect from a man who, but a few days ago, was a total stranger?

Boy, I was mad. Part of my anger stemmed from the fact that I had thought Teppy an innocent type of man. Lovable, if you get what I mean. He had come to our house and eaten of our breakfast and made out that he was such a friend of the Old Man's. But now I knew better. He was the most unkind, cruel, greedy and anti-boy man I had ever run into. Just because he didn't wish to share with me his mush of a dinner – which wasn't even good for decent pigs anyway – he had made up a story that he had been eating snake meat and alligator jowls. He wasn't a friend of the Old Man's at all, or would he blackmail the son? And yet I dared not approach the Old Man about what I had discovered in Teppy. At least not just yet. It would suit me to play this blackmail game. For a while anyway. Until I gathered some clear thoughts.

The jam in which I suddenly found myself had raised my temperature double-quick for although I was standing in the cool, river-freshened air, I was sweating like mad. Boy, boy, boy! That rat.

Just then the Old Man's voice split the Sunday quiet with, 'Beppo!'

Meaning dinner was ready.

I ran down Teppy's decaying steps and made towards the house at a fast clip.

CHAPTER 4

Bullet head-pow!

Monday morning and my first day in school.

The Old Man said he wanted everything good for me. He was going to see that I grew up a Christian and also that I got a good education. So to school with me.

But what a laugh there was when I entered the classroom. The joke was on me, yes sir! Whether in an effort to save money or to avoid sending me to the local barber, or because he believed too much in himself, the Old Man, with shear and razor had transformed my hairy head into virtual baldness. Save for a patch of hair on the plateau of my head it was bald. And shiny. And rugged. I mean the bone structure, now bared of hair, revealed itself unsymmetrical and bumpy.

The barbarism had been performed that very morning. To be sure I had sickened at the sight of it, hopefully praying that my hair, by some magic, would be restored. Immediately. Or that night while I slept. In fewer than thirty minutes before school I must have looked more than a dozen times in the mirror. Now I was confronted by a classful of laughing students. And who could blame them?

Everybody laughed, the boys, of course, outdoing the girls, rolling their heads on their desks and cackling like hyenas. But I was surprised that the girls should have found it so funny as well. Only one of them, a fat youngster, was satisfied with a smile. I thanked her for it. Even the teacher, a prissy type, unable to stifle her laughter, pulled out her handkerchief and covered her face. Full three minutes went by before she brought the class under control and even then there came sporadically a little laughter. But one boy more than all others could not be contained. Time and time again he interrupted the lesson with cannon bursts of giggling.

I soon found that, in addition to being the class's major dunce, he was the school's bully. George Kirby by name.

I would have liked to be seated in the back to escape attention; instead Miss Clemens, the teacher, had a place for me in dead centre.

'Children,' she said, 'our new pupil is Beppo . . .'

More laughter. George Kirby went into fits. Beppo? Beppo? What kind of name was that? He laughed more than the situation demanded.

'. . . Children,' Miss Clemens went on, 'this is no way to carry on. George, I'm ashamed of you! And you, too, Daphne . . . !'

Daphne?

I turned and there she was. The Belmont girl. In the same class. And her name, as Teppy had hinted, was indeed Daphne. But now she made a show of laughing at me, hushing up because the teacher had appealed for clemency towards me, but eyeing me, smiling a little and laughing a little and taking great pains in showing me in what singular high derision she held me. But somehow the blow was softened.

We were in the same class. And I liked the brat. I have always appreciated spunk and she had spunk.

Miss Clemens continued her speech of welcome, expressing the manner in which she expected them to treat me, with kindness and respect until I had adjusted to my new situation. Well, that was that anyhow.

I took my seat and there was the roll call and everybody was present because she commended the class for its good attendance. We soon commenced work. Arithmetic. Long division. Yech!

If the grocer is buying mangoes by the box, each box holding one gross, how many boxes did he buy if altogether he has 1872 mangoes?

N.B. 1 gross = 144.

There were other problems as well but the above showed that she clearly was ahead of the mango season for which she should be commended.

As soon as she had finished setting the work on the blackboard, Miss Clemens seated herself at her desk, busying herself with this and that, but the class knew the system. As soon as they were finished, the students marched up to the desk and had their books marked, some returning with bright happy faces because theirs were right, others with donkey-long ones.

I couldn't keep count of the many times I was patted on my bald head. Some boys went out of their way to pass by my desk and to pat me, each giving me a name or repeating that which had been given by his predecessors.

Egg head.

Big head.

Shiny head.

Bullet head.

Characteristically George Kirby had to beat everyone at this game. Not satisfied with a humble pat, he slapped me on the head with a heavy hand, cupping his fingers around it as though he were grasping a basketball, then he twitched them in. It was a mighty painful blow and snapped like the lash of a whip and everybody laughed. They enjoyed that.

I didn't take that one though, but shot from my seat and grabbed him in the collar. We wrestled, knocking a couple of desks about and, with as much ease as a dog playing with a puppy, he flung me down on the floor and we rolled over and over, but I didn't let go of his collar. I wished I could have let go long enough to salute his buck teeth with a fist when Miss Clemens intervened.

'Stop that, you two!'

We disengaged and his collar slowly unwrinkled itself and I wished to God it was his nose that was coming back into position. I sat down.

'Any more of this nonsense,' the teacher promised, 'and you two will hear from me in a place that will make you hurt.'

I was already hurting. Bruises on my neck and my shank was bleeding. Just a bit. George had won that one and would win the others as well. Unless I used my head.

The class settled again but I could read that I had made giant strides. Obviously in the direction of self-destruction. I had challenged the bully.

If anything, though, most of the class seemed not merely surprised at my courage or naïvety or whatever it was, but genuinely sympathetic. They seemed to be worrying for my fate. They were sure that George would batter me.

Daphne was the only one who seemed pleased. I would be clobbered and battered and she looked forward to it. Curse her.

George constantly gave me a preview of what was in store for me: making a fist and grinding it around in his eye, meaning he was going to black mine.

Daphne was ever so pleased.

We did some reading and then it was recess and the class stampeded for the outdoors and the sunshine, though I deemed it suitable to my condition to walk. No point in racing out there to be bludgeoned. Funny thing, though, I wasn't afraid. No one was on my side and that alone gave me courage. Had I a single friend in that class I would have been afraid, but instead I felt like a martyr about to be stoned or burned and I didn't care. And with my cap on, too, I felt less naked and therefore more secure.

George was waiting. He was with the group. They were standing about thirty yards off on a patch of ground which had been laid bare by hundreds of playing feet. As I emerged from the door and on to the steps, Daphne whispered something to George.

Followed by the others, George came to meet me.

'Say your last prayer,' he said.

'What for?' I asked.

''Cause I going to make you eat dirt,' he said. 'You grabbed me in the collar in class.'

'Sure I grabbed you!'

'Was that a challenge?'

'That was a challenge.'

'For that you will eat dirt,' he said, making fists.

'Oh yes!' I said, as spunky as a Napoleon. I had learnt the way to handle bullies. They are like dogs. Cringe in fear and they bite. But stand firm and they are stupefied. Uncertain. They think you have a secret weapon.

It was the same with bully George Kirby. He was losing some of his belligerence. Faltering. Looking around at his cronies who had gathered and were still gathering.

'Egg head!' he said.

'I'm waiting to eat dirt, George Kirby,' I said, knowing certainly that if he chose to attack I would be mincemeat.

'You take that, George?' Daphne said in a shocked voice. 'I don't believe it.'

'Me neither,' said a boy who was wearing baggy pants and whose head was as bushy as mine was bald.

'I . . . I don't want to hurt him,' George said. 'Miss Clemens will . . . you know what she'll do.'

My tactic was working.

Daphne, however, would have nothing of his foolish talk

which revolved around my welfare and Miss Clemens's strap. She kindly helped him to make up his mind.

She bent down and filled her hand with fine red dust, holding it between us. What a girl! A natural hater. She hated me because I was the Old Man's son and for nothing else. And I wasn't even his son by blood.

'Come on,' she said. 'Come on.'

One of us had to knock the dust in the other's face. The challenge. Since it was evident I couldn't beat George in a fair fight I wouldn't, so it was up to him to do it. And the others gave him little choice.

'Come on, George!'

'Let him eat dirt, George!'

I saw him clearly – taller than I by about three or four inches, his arms long and muscular and reaching nearly down to his knees. A pair of adze-like teeth protruded from his perpetually-open mouth and gave him the look of a retarded boy. I wouldn't want them sunken in my flesh; it would be better to break them off. I knew I'd have to play some trick, if and when he knocked up the dust, just to survive.

But he was on the spot. Was he ever on the spot, sweating as the others egged him on! I didn't take my eyes off his hands at all. Monitoring his movements was important.

There!

He knocked the dust up but I was ready and ducked and in doing so ran at him with my head which now could truthfully be called a bullet.

It not only knocked the breath out of him but toppled him off his feet as well, and before he could get up, I filled my hand with fine earth of the same geological composition as Miss Daphne Belmont had scooped up and with it blinded him.

'What . . . ?' was all he managed as – poor fellow – I

pounded him with my little fists. How I pounded him! On the nose. In the eyes. On the head.

He wallowed around in the red dust, rubbing his eyes to clear them but not succeeding, groaning better than most boars can, and asking where he was. And not a soul laughed at him. So afraid were they of Mr George.

I kicked him in the ribs and on the shanks, he ooing and aaahing and hollering, 'Lord! Lord!' and when I was tired of kicking I jumped up and down on his stomach. I would have gone on and on but somebody pulled me off him, and it was Miss Clemens.

She had heard the commotion, seen the gathering and run out. George was a sight. I couldn't tell the colour of his clothes, they were so red with dust.

Utter shock silenced the crowd. Except for children too small to know what a bully was like and that making fun of him could prove painful, they stood there gaping.

Miss Clemens led us away, especially George who could hardly see where he was going. She made him wash himself in the cistern of the tank, and she took us both inside. Usually there is a trial, the teacher acting the role of judge, determining who started it and so forth, but not so this time. Miss Clemens wanted to know nothing new. She had seen us scrap in class, had warned us and she merely gave us what she had promised us then.

Oh boy, did she ever lay it on! Six in the left hand, five in the right and when I was slowing down in holding out the hand for more she gave me the rest over the body. George got the same treatment, Miss Clemens coughing for all the red dust she was knocking out of his clothes and sucking down into her delicate lungs. There was much pretend crying from both of us for there were no tears.

But what an upset victory I had achieved.

I was instantly aware of the new awe in which I was being

held. Those boys who had gone out of their way to pass by my desk for the sake of patting me on the head, steered a wide berth from now on, even when it was required of them to walk by. Good for that. There was even a hint in the air that old alliances might be crumbling and new ones being considered.

Daphne was so crushed and mad.

For the rest of the morning her mouth remained pouted and I believe she neglected her work because I heard the teacher rebuking her and expressing surprise that her work was so poor.

She refused to look at me, she who had so frequently eyed me with contempt and amusement. She was upset, not so much by the fact that George had been drummed, but because she had forced him into this dishonour that I had wrought to his bully stature.

Already he was swelling over the right eye and a few lumps which we called 'cocoes' had appeared on his forehead. He felt so small, ever so small, and I felt like the giant-killer.

But mine were not all rosy thoughts. I had won by trickery. How would the other round go?

CHAPTER 5

A friend at last

By lunch time my stock had risen pretty fast and I had won myself a friend. Roy Penner. He was the smallest boy in our class.

'Where you from?' he asked.

I told him.

'And you?'

'Portland,' he said, adding that it was in Eastern Jamaica. After a second he asked, 'Do you like it here?'

'You bet, Roy.'

He had somewhat of a rat's countenance that went rather well with his milk-white and small teeth. He was dark-complexioned but smooth. There was not a pimple any-where on that boy's face. Many a girl could covet him for his skin alone, but that alone, as I couldn't see any of them wanting to look like him. His trademark was standing with both his hands so deep in his pockets that the tips of the pockets showed peeping below the cuffs of his shorts. He smelt of urine and I supposed he wet his bed at nights.

'Do you like it here, Roy?' I asked.

'Oh yes. But Mrs Jenkins is cross. Know what I mean? Miserable. She whips me sometimes.'

Maybe that was when he wet himself.

I soon found out that he was attracted to me, not so much because I had dethroned George Kirby, but due to the fact of our being in the same boat, so to speak.

He also was an adoption.

When I use the word adoption I am not doing so in the correct sense, because, in seeking a child to adopt, prospective parents enter into lengthy negotiations and sign papers, and the adopted are usually babies who never or rarely find out whom their true parents are. But not so with Roy and me.

We were given away, so to speak, by a simple word-of-mouth agreement and we knew all right whom our parents were and where was home.

The Old Man had met my father at a cricket match in Santa Cruz and one word having led to another and, according to my father, the Old Man had said: 'I say, Joe, you don't happen to know anyone around here who has a boy he'd like to give away?' Yes, the words 'give away' usually replace nicer ones. Well, my father was having enough trouble feeding and clothing and keeping us in school, working his fingers off, migrating to work in the cane fields of St Elizabeth and Westmoreland. He had been looking forward to such an opportunity to get one of us off his hands and, since the Old Man seemed the right sort of man, kind and understanding, he had mentioned me. The Old Man had come home, looked me over, liked whom he had seen and the deal was clinched. I was packed off the selfsame day. Given away. Regret it? Me? No, sir. A finer man than the Old Man was hard to locate. Just as my father had described him. My new life was heaven to me. From abject poverty a catapult into comparative wealth.

But Roy Penner had been given away under slightly harsher circumstances. His mother had taken him along with farm produce to Kingston with the express hope that, on returning, neither produce nor boy would accompany her home. The produce was sold, Roy was donated. While she was at the Coronation Market on Spanish Town Road in Kingston's West End, she had run into Mrs Jenkins, a widow from our village, who had been on the look-out for

47

such a boy as Roy. Small enough for her to handle, she taking into consideration her advancing age and waning strength. The adoption was swift, a bit swifter than mine, and here was Roy, old man.

With his hands still deep in his pockets, he looked covertly around. 'Were you afraid?' he asked.

'When?'

'When George challenged you.'

'No,' I lied.

'Boy,' he said. 'What a fight. Where'd you learn to fight like that?' Taking his hands from his pockets he did some shadow boxing, saying: 'A pow! A pow! Boy! Where did you learn?'

'I took lessons from a boy in Santa Cruz,' I said, hoping that all this would filter back to George and the others and drive uncommon fear into them. 'I know quite a few tricks,' I added. 'Tricks I didn't use.'

'Want to teach me some?'

I didn't know any so I said, 'Why, are you threatened too?'

'Not really. But I could be in trouble.'

'Why?'

'By talking to you. They're all ganged up.'

'Nonsense,' I said. But he was right because just then we were the centre of attraction. 'Let's go,' I told him and began to walk down the hill from the school and towards our respective homes to eat lunch.

Behind us was a throng but they followed at a respectful distance. Daphne was one of them.

However we reached home without incident.

The Old Man noticed nothing of my bruises and I told him nothing. After lunch I had several looks at myself in the mirror. I had hoped that a few hairs would at least be peeping through, but nothing was happening yet.

With the problem of my bald head and my fight with George, I decided to return to school with as little time to spare as possible. So I timed it right and entered the school yard just when the bell rang for the afternoon session.

Nothing happened during class but by recess I noticed a new development. Nowhere could I find Roy Penner. But I soon found out why he was missing and where he was. He had been 'captured' by Daphne and George who were showering friendship on him and feeding him candies. They were keeping my only friend from me. Isolating me. And they were making sure, too, by having him participate in a game.

I drew nearer.

The game involved a mongoose – the villain – and a hen and her chickens. Naturally George was the mongoose and Daphne the Mother Hen. Among the poor little chickens was Roy, old man.

The mongoose is a burrowing animal which has a soft spot for chicken meat.

The game:

'Chicks, chicks, chicks,' called villain mongoose George Kirby, holding out a hand which was supposed to be full of corn.

'We don't want your corn,' said Mother Hen Daphne, Roy Fenner and other chicks who were standing in a file behind an akimboed mother.

'What fat, fat chicks!' said villain George, jumping to one side, the better to select and snatch one of them.

(The idea was he should catch as many of them as possible and so eliminate them from the game.)

'We don't want your corn,' said Mother Hen and chicks.

So as to block mongoose in his strategy, Mother Hen, of course, jumped in the way, the chickens lining up behind her for protection.

I watched them for a time. They knew that I was watching but pretended as though I wasn't there.

'What are you doing, Roy?' I shouted without knowing why.

The game stopped – brups! All eyes turned on me. I didn't know why I had interfered but I had, and here I would go the whole hog.

'Playing a game,' Roy called back.

'With your friends,' Daphne said, expecting Roy to add that. But he did not.

Jeez, what a devil of a girl! She made me mad.

'That's a sissy game!' I said.

'What?' said Daphne. 'You . . . !' She stamped one foot.

'Call me anything,' I said, 'but that's a sissy game.'

'Keep out of this, Egg head!' said George Kirby.

'Sissy game,' I said, taking a bit of bite out of my voice. 'Look at him!' Daphne said, akimbo and preening around as though she were a peacock or a queen. 'Look at him, the give-away.'

The others laughed.

'What did you say?' I shot back at her.

'You're a give-away I said! You're nobody!' And she stamped another Daphne Belmont foot. 'Your parents gave you away,' she added. And to increase the insult she spat on the ground and swung herself on tip-toe in such a way that her skirt flounced up.

How they laughed.

Boy, was I mad! I felt like running up and beating out her brains and plucking that pony tail from her head.

Roy jumped at her with little fists but he did not hit her. 'What did you say that for?'

'Oh, oh,' said George Kirby. 'We forgetting about him. Two of a kind. Another give-away boy.'

I was deeply hurt but could find nothing to say. The other

children kept out of it too. They were mainly riffraff led by these two school viragos, laughing whenever anything, anything at all, was said about us, but saying nothing of their own. Leslie Barber, Sonia Thompson, Mark Dunn, Leona Perez . . . . the lot of them. Even Marcia Donaldson, a fat girl who preferred to live in and by herself, rarely associating with others. But she was with them now. And laughing. Well, smiling.

Roy was sufficiently hurt too, hurt enough to abandon his silly status as a chick in the now-stalled game. With his hands deep in his pockets he walked slowly over and joined me. He would have liked to pout but his mouth – being more rodent-like than snouty – did not lend itself to this kind of action. As he joined me they began, at the instigation of Daphne, the brains of the group, to chant:

> *Their parents gave them away!*
> *They're poor as a church mouse!*
> *Their parents gave them away!*
> *Poor as a church mouse!*

Singing has always appealed to children, and the younger and sillier they are, the deeper the attraction. Their little chant soon paid off handsomely, disrupting other games around the playground and drawing new members. Soon the volume of the thing was even worse than the words. And they had even added a refrain.

> *Their parents gave them away!*
> *Poor as a church mouse!*
> *Poor as a church mouse!*
> *Poor as a church mouse . . . !*

Listening with fever-heat but taking it like a man. That was my way. But Roy began to cry. It was the strangest thing to see this boy cry. The normal child, who does not have to unconsciously cultivate a trademark, gets his hands around the regions of his face in general and the eyes in particular in order to hide such sissy stuff; but not Roy. His hands remained stiffly in his pockets while the silver tears rolled down his cheeks.

I had an idea.

I would have to drive a wedge between George and Daphne and everything, no doubt, would crumble. I would start a chant of my own.

> *Daphne is George Kirby's girl friend!*
> *Daphne is George Kirby's girl friend!*

With the din they were making I am sure they couldn't have heard a word that I was saying but they knew that I was retaliating. Daphne hushed them. All the time Daphne.

I repeated the chant.

When she heard what I was saying, she screamed: 'What?'

Frankly, I had never before seen a girl so horrified. Her eyes doubled size and she went limp.

'Jeez!' said some of her girl friends.

'It's not true,' Daphne said. 'You . . . !'

I chanted:

> *Daphne is George Kirby's girl friend!*
> *Isn't that a funny thing . . . ?*

The other boys began to laugh, much to the embarrassment of George. As for Daphne, she went away, supported by most of her girl friends, went away to cry her dear heart out. Served her right.

The boys milled around George, laughing, patting him

on the shoulder in the way of congratulations for his good fortune with Daphne, but he soon recovered sufficiently from his shock to snap at them and you should have seen those boys shut up mighty fast and saunter off to safer distances.

'Watch what you say about me, you give-away,' George said to me, but he showed no belligerence. If anything he seemed confused.

> *Daphne is George Kirby's girl friend!*
> *Isn't that a funny thing?*

When he realized that for as long as he was prepared to call me a give-away I would chant his name in courting rank with that of Daphne, he merely said, and quite lamely at that: 'You lying . . . !'

I didn't take it any farther because I had achieved my aim and from now on Daphne might be afraid of being seen with George. And of course the fact still remained that George could whip me, only he didn't know it. If he were teased into severe anger he might attack me blindly. When you know that you don't take unnecessary chances.

Roy Penner was heartened by my style and strategy. He was drying his tears.

'What're you crying for?' I asked.

'I didn't like what they said.'

'Nevertheless you can't cry like this at each little setback! Are you a cry baby?'

'No. But I'm not as tough as you.'

It was so good to hear him say that.

I said, 'That's true, Roy. Cry if you want to.'

CHAPTER 6

The Lord's Comin' Soon

But with all my success against my classmates I was sobered by the fact that there was still Teppy to deal with. Two crayfish and a couple of birds to be delivered each week. He hadn't stipulated on what days they be delivered, only that they were. So I had all week in which to work something out.

I dared not tell Roy about the circumstances that involved me in the blackmail. He wouldn't have understood. He might even get it into his rat-like head that I liked Daphne, which might even be very true. But you can't let those smallfry boys into such big mysteries. Yet I had to seek his help.

He helped me put the catapult together.

'You'll need two strips of rubber,' he said. 'From the inner tube of a car or truck.'

'But where? The Old Man has neither car nor truck.'

'Danny Robson has rubber. He's the one to see.'

'Who's this Danny Robson?' I asked.

'He's in standard five,' he said.

'In our school?'

'Sure,' Roy said. 'A short, stout boy with a brush-top type head.'

Seemed to me that heads were the in-things for identifying people in that school.

'I don't know him,' I said.

'I do.'

'Good,' I said.

'It will cost you three pence,' Roy said.

'What?'

Roy shrugged his shoulders, never, never, however, removing his hands from pocket-depth.

'This Danny Robson's a highway robber,' I said. But I had three pence and gave them to Roy to purchase the rubber.

Later that day, with the tongue of an old shoe for the sling and a guava stick that branched like a capital Y we put the catapult together.

So far so good. But there was still the matter of obtaining a fishpot. That night I broached the subject to the Old Man.

'Do you like fish, Dad?'

'What kind, Beppo?'

'Crayfish.'

'Oh, I don't mind 'em at all.'

'You eat them often, Dad?'

'Not often, Beppo.'

'Wouldn't you like to?'

'Why?' He lifted his eyes from the book he was reading and peered at me over the rims of his spectacles. His pipe was in his hand.

'I thought you liked them, sir.'

'But I do.'

'Jeez, Dad. Every boy has a fish-pot.'

'Every boy?'

'Every respectable boy.'

Roy was the only one I knew who had one.

'So?' asked the Old Man, diligently returning to his book.

'Can I have one?'

'Nonsense,' he snorted. 'They're too much trouble. You buy them today and lose them tomorrow. Suddenly there's a rainstorm and they're gone, washed away. It's like throwing money away.'

'But I'll know when it's going to rain!' I said.

'You know when it's going to rain!' He laughed, holding his pipe in a cupped hand. 'The best of us men don't know for sure. You go to bed and all seems hail and hearty and you wake up to thunder and lightning and buckets of rain.'

'Jeez.'

I tried another tack.

'I've made a good friend at school,' I said.

'Good for you.'

'He's small and very smart and he's the outdoors type.'

'Who's he?' asked the Old Man without leaving his book.

'Roy Penner. D'you know him, Dad?'

He looked up. 'He wouldn't be the tyke at Mrs Jenkins's, would he?'

'So you know him?' I said. 'Isn't he real cute?'

'Glad to know you get along, son. He seems lonely. But watch it, Beps. He's a sneaky one, I hear.'

'It's not true.'

'A real prankster they say.'

'He's so quiet,' I said.

'Quiet rivers run deep,' the Old Man said.

I jumped at the word 'river'.

'He has a fish-pot,' I said.

'Oh, not again!'

'Can I have one?'

'To put it this way, Beppo, there's nobody to make it. Joe Rainer's the only one who knows how and he's in jail.'

'Jail!' I said. 'What'd he do?'

'Who, Joe Rainer? Beat up a man as usual. That's his hobby – beating up people. Broke the fellow's arm, split his lip and left him any amount of bruises and wails. But tell you what. There's another man who sometimes passes through here with bamboo baskets and fish-pots. If he does again, Beppo, maybe you'll have one.'

'Hurray!' I said, clapping my hands together.

'But I can't guarantee that he will in another six months, or year,' my Old Man added.

'Rats!' I said.

In the meantime I would have to work out a plan with Roy, such a plan in which he'd supply me two mountain crayfish per week – at a fee of course. For he kept a fish-pot and, to quote him, he got some good and worthy fish and sometimes eels, in the pools. According to a sworn statement of his, Mrs Jenkins, his foster-mother, even with her kind of belligerence, could be soothed by the sight of a huge crayfish or flapping eel. Roy said that on more than one occasion he had avoided a sound thrashing just by taking home some river goodies. He said that they came in so handy that, instead of taking them home in the mornings he had often delayed, bringing them home only when he was sure he would be set upon. According to him he practised these manipulations whenever he had a mind to spend an entire day shooting birds in the bushes or digging for wild yams or bathing in the river. Sometimes, he said, he and his friends spent half a day damming a pool up then baling out another downstream, catching all the fish; this, of course, being done in the dry season when the river was real low. Sometimes it was a game of cricket that stole his time. But whatever it was he'd take home some fish and Mrs Jenkins would be more pleased than mad and in this way he avoided being thrashed.

It was for two things exactly that I coveted Roy. Not for his looks, which weren't something to write home about, but because he owned a fish-pot which enabled him to catch good fish and 'pay' for borrowed time, and he was such a crack catapult shot.

He had begun to give me lessons in the latter art and I was improving, too. My first shot inexplicably landed about ten yards in front of me instead of on a tree top on the green mango against which it had been aimed. But although my second attempt flew three feet wide of the mark, it went up and was a surface-to-air shot, not a surface-to-surface one. I was improving. I might soon be able to shoot a bird. As a matter of fact I had to do it before the week was out and shoot two – not just one. In the meantime, under some pretext or other, I would purchase fish from Roy, using them to pay off Teppy.

During the night it occurred to me that if I were exceedingly nice to the Old Man, he might go out of his way to get me a fish-pot, so instead of sleeping like a log, I woke several times during the night, hoping to wake with the dawn. And I did just that.

'Hey,' he said when he found me up and waiting in the kitchen, the fire made, his coffee pot already zinging with heating water, 'you're up early, Beppo.'

'Oh, I couldn't sleep, sir.'

'Troubles?'

I laughed. 'Troubles, sir? None in the world. I'm really an early riser. Nobody has to wake me in the mornings. These two past mornings, well – I was tired.'

'Is that so? I'm mighty glad to hear that. We'll milk the cows first. What you say to that?'

'Suits me, sir. But wouldn't you care for a cup of coffee?'

He smiled. 'No milk to put in it, Beppo.'

'True, sir.'

'We'll milk the cows.'

I was happy. It seemed my plan had started to work. His benevolent smile assured me it must be working. I would impress him so well that he would ask me if I wished a favour or something and then I'd ask for that fish-pot.

Gaily I milked away but there was a slight setback. For the second morning in a row the milk I obtained from Mabel was half what it had been the first morning I had milked her.

'Founny,' said the Old Man. 'Mable isser bettor milk'r'n that.' He removed his pipe so he could speak clearly. 'That cow's scrub but she's good for four quarts at least.'

'I know, sir. That's what she gave on Sunday when I first milked her.'

'Strange, yes!'

I didn't care to say it but I said it anyhow.

'You think she's withholding the milk from me, sir?'

'Nonsense.'

'Because I'm a new milker or something?'

'There's no cow that can do that, son. She must be getting dry.'

I looked at her calf, still very young, too young for the mother to be losing her grip on milk production. But I said nothing more. This was going against my plan. If I were interfering with milk production? It wasn't that good an impression I was making on the Old Man, was it?

Just then Teppy stepped into view, leaving a trail of smoke puffs behind him and bringing a powerful odour of perspiration and tobacco. He was dressed in his weekday clothes which meant a whole lot of patches and a squished cap that had obviously weathered countless rainstorms.

'Mornin', Tate.'

'Hi ya, Teppy.'

'Nice mornin',' he said, looking around at the clear blue sky and sucking up the mint-fresh sweetness of the morning. 'Hullo, boy,' he said, glancing at me without keeping his eyes on.

'Beppo,' the Old Man said, correcting him.

'Then mornin', Beppo,' he said, maliciously, but avoiding my eyes; ashamed, no doubt, of holding me to blackmail.

'Hi,' I said. Dropping his name from the salutation was more formal.

'A funny thing's been happening,' the Old Man said. 'Suddenly Mabel won't give any milk.'

'Not any! How you mean, Tate?' asked Teppy, looking at anything but the Old Man -- the sunshiny hills and the trees and happy-go-lucky birds.

'Mabel's a four-quarter, Teppy. But suddenly she's been giving less. And much less.'

'What?' But to me his countenance didn't assume sufficient shock proportion to match the way he had said, *What?*

'She been giving two quarts or so these past mornings.'

I knew it. He looked at me; Teppy, that is.

'Who's been milkin' 'er?' he asked.

'That has nothing to do with it, Teppy.'

'The boy's respons'ble,' Teppy said. ' 'E don' know nothin' 'bout milkin' that cow.'

'Nonsense,' said the Old Man.

''Ave it your way, Tate.'

'You're always picking on Beppo,' the Old Man said. 'What is it, you don't like him?'

'I do, I do,' he said. ''E's a nice boy an' all an' very clever. I like 'im like 'e was me own.'

Liar!

He went on. 'But it sure is a funny thing wit' the cow. Could be the Lord is comin' soon to claim 'is worl', Tate. For it mus' be somethin' like that. They's all kinds o' strange happenin's goin' on. Jus' yesterday I 'eard of a cow givin' birt' to triplets. You ever 'eard o' triplets bein' distri-booted among cow-kin' before? No, sir. Triplets? Mercy! An' they's talk of a two-head dog over in Lucea. Strange things goin' on in Nature, Tate. Mysterious things. Everything's topsy-turvy. Your cow sudd'n'ly becomin' half the cow she used to be, givin' two quarts instead o' four! The

Lord's comin' soon, Tate. Mark me words. 'E spoke in visions an' t'rough prophets an' now 'E's speakin' in cows. The worl's comin' sholy to an end.'

And with no further word Teppy tepped away.

Looking at him limp away, the Old Man shook his head. 'That's Teppy for you. Every dadburn thing's got some heavenly meaning. The philosophy matches the man.'

'Which is just like rags,' I said suddenly.

'Oh-Oh! Watch your words, son. Whatever he is he is still an adult.'

Adult blackmailer.

I had the feeling he had made up those stories about the cow that gave birth to triplets, especially the one about the two-headed dog. By mentioning them he hoped to strengthen his arguments that strange things were happening, even to Mabel. This business of the milk was indeed strange but it couldn't be explained in Teppy's way. I couldn't see what God could have to gain by speaking through Mabel. No way!

I had the strange feeling that there was a lot more to Teppy than met the eyes, an unknown quantity in the man. Something in addition to his being a blackmailer.

In his short discourse with the Old Man he had looked at me no more than once. Perhaps he was ashamed of the way he had acted with me. Perhaps it was for something else. For I wasn't quite sure that he was the type to meet up with shame and recognize it. How could I know what lay buried deep inside that rascally man?

Anyway, inexplicably, by the next morning, Mabel's milk supply went up. Not to what it used to be. Not the four quarts; she gave about three. Maybe God had decided to speak less through her.

CHAPTER 7

Face to face with Boadicea

We let the cows and calves loose in the pasture with the others, and the Old Man let me go to attend to the goats.

There were five of them and one of them was mine. A gift from Dad. A young she-goat which I had named Mavis; she sported a major colour of brown interspersed with white. She was beautiful and even seemed intelligent.

In that they are madly nomadic, goats are troublesome. They will pass up good juicy wild herbs and bush to feed on the neighbours' young banana sprouts or tender yam vines, which can mean a whole lot of trouble. A good neighbour might just raise a ruckus, a bad one will impound the animal, the real mean one slit the throat of the intruder.

Mrs Belmont being our neighbour whom we could not classify as being good, and having yams and bananas on her property, we were taking care. What other choice had we? So every one of the flock of five goats was kept tethered in ropes down near the river where grew an assortment of edible runners and bush. Save when it looked like rain they were not taken home at nights. Then they were driven up and into the buggy house.

But when I reached the spot where they had been left for the night, Mavis was not there. All the others were except Mavis. My goat.

Before I looked around, Mavis bleated: a pristine, throaty cry. And, Lord! The bleat came from the direction of the Belmont property. She must have seen or heard me, but as yet I could not see her. I ran around the bush that stood in my way and there she was, tethered short on a small stake, and by her side stood Daphne Belmont.

Hell's bells! Daphne. Now I had it coming.

My first reaction was one of fear but I applied control quickly. Mavis had not been killed. That was the main thing. She had merely been impounded.

I needed some time to think and began to pace the grass, walking back and forth. Should I call the Old Man?

But why?

This was Daphne Belmont holding my goat in custody, not her mother. She was my age, by George, why should I call an adult to deal with a child? I'd handle it myself. Maybe with a little diplomacy.

But that Daphne, she wasn't even looking at me! With folded arms she looked the other way. Crisp miss! That girl really meant business.

'Hello there!'

'Don't hello me!' she shouted back. Under her breath she added: 'Fresh!'

'Did my goat bother you?'

'Did your goat bother me?' she mimicked. 'What do you think she came over for? To pay me a visit? To stand around?'

Brother!

'What did it eat?'

'She's in deep trouble,' she said, looking at tree tops.

All this conversation so far had taken place with her back to me. Mavis was chewing a comfortable cud.

'May I come over and see?'

'I ought to shoot you but you may.'

Progress is progress anyway one might look at it. But before I progressed over to her property, for some reason or other, my eyes caught the severed rope and, to my dis-belief, found that Mavis had not, in straining on it, broken the rope. After all, it was almost brand-new. It had been severed! Cut! With a sharp instrument, a machete or a knife. By whom else but by Daphne? Good grief. The girl was Boadicea herself. This was her way of getting back at me for teasing about George being her boy friend. If you can't catch Harry then you catch his shirt.

However, I didn't betray my knowledge about the rope and decided I'd keep quiet about it and play the ball game her way until I couldn't any longer. But it was clear to me I'd have to handle her with kid gloves.

I climbed through the barbed wire fence where it was most in a state of deterioration and where both Mavis and Daphne must have passed, and quickly got to where they were standing.

Like myself Daphne was bare-footed. Like me, too, she had passed through much dew. The hem of her dress was a light grey and drooping unfashionably from the dew's wet-ness, her feet shiny wet.

'Hi,' I said. 'I'm here.'

'Hi yourself.'

'I'm really sorry about the goat, Daphne.'

'Daphne's for me and my friends.'

'What should I call you then?'

'Call me nothing.'

At a glance I examined this end of the rope and noted that Daphne Boadicea Belmont had done a capital job in pounding the sliced end to make it into a fuzzy, natural-looking break. Too bad for her that she had overlooked the other end. My trump. To be played later. If necessary. After all, if I exposed her as the devil she was acting, I'd really shame her to high heaven and we might never get on speak-ing terms.

'Well, what damage did she do?'

She turned on me. 'What damage? All over!'

I couldn't see any. And I was sure there wasn't any because the goat had been brought here by her.

'All over where?' I asked. 'I don't see any.'

As if in agreement Mavis bleated.

But Daphne was in aggressive mood.

'How can you see when you're blind, blind, blind!' Each 'blind' being accompanied by a mighty stamp of foot. 'It ate our plants all over,' she said. 'Not in one place, dummy!'

I didn't like being called a dummy at all, but when your hand is in the tiger's mouth, you take your time and slip the ruddy thing out. Yes, sir.

And she went on: 'And what of the trouble it gave me to catch? Hauling and pulling me!'

I could have said, This small goat hauled and pulled you? But instead I said, 'I'm sorry.'

'Sorry!' Very scornfully. 'Then look sorry!'

She was something else.

'I ought to have taken her to my mom.'

'Thanks for not doing that, Daphne.'

'And you're so fresh.' She stole a glance at me.

'Am I?'

'And stupid.'

Another glance stolen.

'Me stupid?'

'You and your Mr Tate. You're both the stupidest people I know.'

A rebuking look.

'I don't believe it. He's not stupid. Dad's a sensible man.'

'Oh yes,' she said, pointing a finger, 'then how come he doesn't know what's going on on his place?'

'He doesn't?'

What foolish talk.

'Nor do you know,' she said.

'What's going on. Of course we know. We do our house-work and all the farm jobs. Of course we know what's going on.'

'Oh yes?'

'What's going on then that we don't know of?'

'If you do know, bright boy, why ask me?'

She irritated me. She was just making talk. Or . . . Was she referring to the fact that she had sliced my rope in two? I'd let her know. But I checked myself. Better let it go.

'May I take my goat and go?'

'After you apologize.'

'Apologize! For what? For a goat?'

'For what you said about George Kirby and me.' She swung at me as if to hit me. 'You think I could like that dunce and hulk!'

'Good.'

It wasn't intentional. The blooming word slipped out.

'What's good, you fool?'

'Nothing.' I even smiled. Being called a fool and smiling.

'Well, are you going to apologize?'

'Only when you do, Daphne. After all, you said some pretty nasty things about me, too. Sometimes I think you hate me.'

'I do!'

'You hate me?'

'Of course I do! Everybody knows that.'

'I didn't know.'

'Because you're stupid.'

'About the goat,' I said.

'Take it and go! Your wishy-washy goat!'

'Thanks,' I said. 'See you in school.'

'Bleah!' she said.

I took Mavis and went down the hill back to our land,

Mavis bleating happy little bleats in her throat. *Meh-eh-eh* and *Meh-eh-eh*.

Daphne made a great show of stamping off but I could feel her eyes on me. From behind a banana tree perhaps. When I got to the fence I looked back. Got her too! She was watching me all right. She swung around fast and stamped away, her wet skirt doing its best at flouncing but only swinging heavily.

Not a bad kid, that Daphne. Spunky, quite spunky. And tricky too.

But this time we had played to a draw.

I wondered what she meant by saying that neither the Old Man nor I knew what was going on. She couldn't have meant the rope because the Old Man wasn't involved. It was something else and might even be important. But what?

CHAPTER 8

What do you say to God?

School was normal. Nothing of note happened.

Little hairs were peeping through my scalp again but nevertheless I felt awfully naked. Nobody, however, bothered me any more.

Daphne's and my eyes met more than a few times each day in class and, though she cut them at me and held her head rather belligerently, the whole thing seemed pitifully watered down. Each time our eyes met I smiled at her and she resisted but I was sure that, on one occasion when she bent her head on top of the desk, she was sharing a smile with that cold, impersonal board.

George Kirby and I had no clashes. Not even with eyes. He was keeping away from me. Like the plague. I liked that.

There was only one laugh at my expense and it had nothing to do with my head.

For the benefit of slower students including George, Miss Clemens had put an addition problem on the blackboard. They were supposed to add as she pointed out the numbers. The others of us were expected to be occupied with problems of our own but I couldn't help watching. I am a natural watcher. As she added the first column and the group said 22, she wrote down a 2, carrying the other 2 to the tens column and writing it over the top in this manner:

$$2$$
$$7521$$
$$3416$$
$$5524$$
$$1137$$
$$1224$$
$$\overline{}$$
$$2$$

As soon as she began to point out the tens column from the top, she saying 2 plus 2, I hollered out, 'Blackmail!' So much was I thinking of the two fish plus two birds which Teppy had demanded, that I shouted the word involuntarily.

Everybody turned and everybody laughed. Even Roy gave it to me. I felt silly all right.

'Two plus two equals blackmail,' said Daphne scornfully. 'Now I've heard of everything. Silly dunce!'

'Beppo Tate,' Miss Clemens said with extraordinary anger. 'Any more of your comedy, my man, and I'll comedy your rump!'

What could I say? She was in her rights. Blackmail! I was under pressure all right. That Teppy, I'd get him some day.

Roy ran to me at recess.

'What did you say such a fool thing for?' He laughed rat's teeth. 'Two plus two equals blackmail! Boy, you're funny.'

No point in rejecting the compliment so I said, 'That class could use some good belly laughs every day. It's getting dull in there, don't you see?'

'You're too much for me.'

'Somebody's got to liven things up.'

'Yes, sir.'

'It's your turn tomorrow to provide the laugh,' I said.

'Oh no. Not me. One more foolish crack like that and Miss Clemens is going to burn up the person's back pocket with her strap, Dr Do-Good. Not me, old man.'

'Ah well,' I said. 'I guess I'm the only clown.'

But he was very impressed with my ability to entertain. That afternoon, after school, he invited me to accompany him to set his fish-pot.

It was made of bamboo slats, the fish-pot, and shaped like a corn-on-the-cob, only fatter at the big end. The latter end was furnished with a funnel-shaped opening – the entrance – where fish entered at their perilous will, while the thin end held the exit now corked tight with a bundle of thrash, and through which the trapped fish, after a respectful wait, were allowed out and into cooking pots.

First Roy baited it carefully with powerful-smelling roast coconut flesh.

'This will attract them from a mile away,' he said.

'You can say that again.'

'Roast coconut and jackfruit are among the best baits,' he assured me.

I knew jackfruit, an offensive-smelling though sweet pulpy fruit, large as a melon, pimpled on the outside and growing on a tree.

Since, with the right kind of luck I might soon be a fisherman also, I watched intently and listened carefully to the artist.

'What are those for?' I asked him of the broken crockery which were in the pot.

'Oh. To attract fish. See, they're white!'

'Right.'

'Fish are attracted to bright things.'

'And the stones?'

'Sinkers.'

'You make me seem a simpleton, Roy.'

'You'll learn,' said Roy, the face of his cap almost hiding his eyes. 'Let's go.'

We tramped along the river bank, among lush marigold plants profusely in flower, walked past tall bamboos that swayed with every breath of restless wind and alongside dwarf coco plants clustering together in colonies, their broad leaves forming umbrellas.

A woodpecker was drilling a home somewhere.

Finally we came to a pool which was very much longer than it was broad and Roy said:

'Here it is.'

'Is it a good place?'

'It never fails,' he said.

'Big ones?'

'Sometimes.'

The fish-pot was equipped with a leash and Roy threw the pot from his hand to land swishing into the water. It sank slowly and correctly, meaning that it went down horizontally. He tied the leash to a small tree.

'That's it.'

'I wish I had one,' I said.

'Prod Marse Tate,' said Roy.

He called my Dad Marse instead of Mister.

'I'll have to do that, Roy. But I don't know. He didn't seem too interested.'

'Keep at him. It's the only way. Break him down.'

'I guess you're right.'

We walked away from the river through thick grass until we hit a little-used footpath.

'Where are we going?' I asked Roy.

'You'll see.'

We were going away from the village, deeper and deeper into the woods, then suddenly we came upon a small hut which was built on an A frame of rose apples and bamboo spars and thatched with dry cane leaves. It was fairly well hidden under the trees. He led me right in as though he owned it.

'Whose hut is this?' I asked. 'Mrs Jenkins's?'

'Nope.'

'Whose then?'

'Mine.'

He owned it.

'Boy!' was all I said, but it was coated in envy.

Looking around I saw a fireplace of three stones set in a crude circle and with extinguished firewood still in it. In one corner was more firewood and also a basket-ball-sized breadfruit, very fit, the ones they set aside for roasting. On the dirt floor to one side was a layer of dry banana leaves that seemed at some time to be used as a bed.

Nonchalantly, as though this was a natural thing for a boy to own, Roy went about his business, unpocketing a small box of matches. He proceeded to light a fire.

'What're you doing?' I asked, almost alarmed.

'I'm going to roast me a breadfruit,' he said. 'That one.' With his mouth he pointed out the one I have already described. 'It won't take long. But if you don't care to wait, I'll see you tomorrow.'

'But . . .'

He set some dry thrash in the fireplace and over it the fire-sticks, then he struck a match and the fire was lit.

'Jeez!' I said, sitting down on the dry banana leaves. 'Do you come here often?'

'Often enough.'

'And you built it?'

'Who else, old man?'

'Boy, you're a deep one all right. You're deeper than I ever could imagine.'

'Sometimes I cook here,' he said, pointing out a soot-blackened tin pan which hung from a rafter of the hut on a wire handle.

'Cook here? What for?' I was amazed. This boy looked puny and of no account but he knew how to live. 'Won't Mrs Jenkins miss you today?'

'Nope. She's gone visiting. She has a sister down the road about two miles. Smoke?' he asked.

'Smoke?'

This time I was truly appalled.

'Why not?' said cool boy Roy.

'What're you talking about?'

'A smoke,' he said with a straight rat's face.

He brought out from his pocket a folded paper which he undid, tearing it in two and handing me a half. Without further explanation he began to roll his part of the paper into a cigarette. I was so thoroughly amazed that I merely sat there looking at him until, taking a twig from the fire, he lit it. He knew how to conserve matches when there was a roaring fire at hand.

But I couldn't take it any more. I burst out laughing and rolling on the dry leaves.

'What're you laughing at, old man?'

'Boy, you're a wonder all right. You give me nice sensations in my belly parts.'

'Come on,' he said. 'Try it.'

Calmly he set the breadfruit atop the three stones and over the fire which was crackling in earnest.

'Try it,' he went on, puffing on his paper cigarette.

Well, I'd be doggoned. Anyway I didn't see how any harm could have come from my trying it, nor was I convinced that I would be committing a wrong. After all it was a pure paper cigarette and this was all pretend smoking. So I rolled her up and, fixing it in my mouth at a rather rakish angle, lit up.

My first smoke and at the instigation of puny Roy. But at the first pull I choked and coughed.

'Wow!' I said. The smoke itself seemed a bit warm for the tongue. At least my tongue.

'You'll get used to it, old man,' Roy said, reclining on his back and pulling one leg up under him, resting the other over the knee of the first. 'It took me a while to get used to,' he added.

'You certainly know how to live,' I said. 'You know I covet you. I'm really beholding to you, Roy, I mean I'm glad you like me and take me as a friend. Do I envy you?'

'Me?' he said, taking his eyes from the ceiling and looking at me with restrained shock. 'Look who's talking! I wish I was in your shoes.'

'What do you mean?'

'I mean, man, I wish Marse Tate was the one who had taken me.'

'Why?'

''Cause he's a better man than that Mrs Jenkins.'

'She's not a man,' I said.

'Ah, you know what I mean,' he said. 'He feeds you good, don't he?'

'He does, sure he does.'

'Rice-and-peas and ackees and cod fish and pork chops, good beef, liver and fish and the works, right?'

'Right.'

''Cause I can smell it clear to here sometimes. What a man to cook!'

'Yes, he's jolly good, Roy. But what are you getting at?'

'I mean that my tongue is longing out of my head for some of that food, old man. Nothing less.'

'But . . .'

'I don't get all those good things to eat! Leastways not often.'

'What do you get to eat then, Roy?'

'Corned pork mostly and tripe, tripe, tripe.'

'Tripe?'

'Yes. Hog guts. Goat guts. Cow guts. Three times a week sometimes. I'm sick, up to here.' He indicated that he was sick up to his ruddy throat.

'Oh.'

I was sorry to learn of his plight.

'And even when I bring home good fish, old man, something fresh, something different, a welcome change, that doggone woman is likely to sell them.'

'Sell them? That's bad.'

'Sure she sells them. If she gets the buyer. That woman is deadly against good food. I seen her sell to Marse Tate and the shopkeeper, that big belly Mr Ebenezer. I could kill her.'

'Oh. Too bad.'

He took a giant puff.

'You don't know that woman. That's why I built the hut and cook here when I get the chance to.'

He smoked steadily, much like a professional. I had to be satisfied with the occasional puff, choking on each puff of smoke that invaded my lungs. But I felt great as though I was in the court of a prince. The prince of rebels and innovations.

The fire continued its happy crackling, blackening the face of the breadfruit deeper and deeper.

After a while Roy asked, 'What do you pray at nights, Beppo?'

'What do I pray for at nights or what do I pray?'

'What do you say to God?'

This boy was amazing. What he said made me swallow. He was deeper, much deeper than the average boy. Snatching the occasional smoke and cooking out here in his hut could well fall within the framework of an ordinary boy's life, but what did he want with religion as well?

'What do I say to God?' I repeated, trying hard to think of a suitable answer, something profound enough for him and a confirmation of my religious wisdom.

'Do you ask for anything?' he went on. 'I mean, old man, do you make up your own prayer?'

'Sure, I make up my own prayer. Last night for instance I asked for that fish-pot I need so badly.'

'And you'll get it, too, because that's clean plain asking. And they say that God is a willing listener if you have something to say, especially something new. Me? I got to say the same fool prayer night after night.'

'You got to be joking. How's that?'

'How's that is right. Mrs Jenkins's orders, old man. Every night she comes to my room to see me off. "Say your prayers, boy," she barks in her flat voice. So I got to kneel down, close my blinking eyes and say the same thing.'

'What kind of prayer is that?' I asked.

'Good question,' he said, shooting smoke from his mouth. 'The forever prayer shall we say?'

We laughed.

'But what is it?'

'Wait till you hear it, old man.'

'Shoot, man.'

'H'mm!' Then:

> *Pray momma*
> *Pray papa*
> *Pray to God*
> *To bless me*
> *And make me*
> *A good little boy.*

Good grief. The words were funny enough but it was the mimicry in his voice that made it double hilarious.

'You've got to say that?'

'Every night, old man.'

It must have bothered him, too, he was puffing wildly.

'But that's ridiculous, Roy!'

'You can say that again.'

I was sorry for him. Mrs Jenkins was not only old in years but ancient in her ideas. Certainly she was behind the times. Poor Roy. Trouble with his food and problems with prayers.

I didn't think Mrs Jenkins treated him first class. He worked hard like a horse and now he was complaining about food. She must have just wanted a slave, not a boy she could call her own. With me it was different. Already I had assumed the Old Man's surname. I was Beppo Tate at school and everywhere, although it was not yet official. Name changes as other government business take one heck of a time usually. But Roy was with his foster mother for full three years and he was still the same old Roy Penner, not Roy Jenkins.

His bed was nothing to write home about either. No mattress filled with fine bed grass as mine was. His was a lot of old rags thrown over bed laths. That was something I had left behind.

He sat up and turned the other cheek of the breadfruit – since we are on the subject of religion – to the fire.

'How do you like smoking?' he asked.

'First class,' I said.

'I love it,' he said. 'Perks a fellow up.'

I was about to ask, 'Smoking paper?' but I let it be. He had enough troubles without having his beliefs shot down.

After a while he said: 'Another thing I can't stand with that Mrs Jenkins. She whipped me yesterday 'cause I said,

77

"Hell, where's my catapult?" She claimed I was swearing. How come,' he asked, 'that she can use the word and I can't?'

'I don't know, Roy. Old women are strange people. How does she use it?'

'Well, she's always yelling at me. Either that I'm the devil in hell or that I'm going to go there sure as hell when I die.'

'Old people've got privileges, Roy.'

'Privileges my granny! I'm going to hell and she's going to heaven. How you like that?'

'Who, Mrs Jenkins going to heaven?'

'Leastways that's what she says. That the good Lord's preparing a place for her in heaven.'

'Oh.'

'I think she's right at that. If she's thinking of going there with her tainted meat the good Lord's bound to prepare a place for her. A special corner.'

I laughed. 'Is her meat tainted?'

'Jeez, what you think I'm complaining about, old man?' Amazing, amazing.

'And there's the other thing. If heaven is opposite to hell, how come you can say heaven night and day and you can't say hell any time.'

This boy was deep, deep, deep, rock-bottom deep.

'I don't know, Roy. Maybe it's a bad place, that's why.'

'That's what they say.' He waited. 'You know, bad or not, I'd rather go there. I don't want to meet up with Mrs Jenkins in heaven. No way. She'd spoil it anyway. I wonder if she thinks there's any tripe up there.'

We cackled.

Deeper than deep.

I was happy when he shifted from religion and his foster mother because on the former subject he was making me look like a novice. He waited a minute then he said:

'Do you like girls, Beppo?'

'Yes,' I said.

A pleasant change of subject. Quite deep too.

'They're crazy,' he said. 'Would you let a girl kiss you?'

'I don't know.'

'How come you don't know that?'

I gave it some hurried thought and said, 'I guess not, Roy.'

'Good.'

'I don't see why a boy should allow that.'

'Right,' he said.

'I think he's the one to make the move and kiss the dad-burn girl.'

'What?' He just about jumped into the fire. 'You'd . . .' he swallowed. '. . . kiss . . .' Another swallow. '. . . a girl?'

'Why not?'

'My God,' he said, turning his attention to the fire. A minute passed. 'You'd kiss Daphne?'

'Why Daphne?'

'Well, would you?'

'How would I know? And we're enemies too.'

'But would you if you were . . . well, on good terms?'

'What are we talking about such nonsense for anyway?'

Actually I liked what he was saying. Continue, Roy.

'That Daphne is crazy,' he observed.

'Yes? And why, my man?'

'No offence meant, pardie.'

'Offence?' I asked. 'I hate that girl.'

'You know, George Kirby was going to beat the day-lights out of me! He started with pelting me in the head with his big fingers, saying that I was your footstool and all because you and I are friends. So, Daphne came right up, prim and womanly as you please, and ordered him to leave me alone.'

'She did that?'

79

'Sure, she did. She's crazy. And she wasn't even talking to me before. She's crazy, old man.'

'When was this, Roy?'

'Today. On my way back to school from lunch.'

'I see,' I said. But it intrigued and pleased me. Something had begun to happen. Definitely. Daphne was changing attitude. Due to my goat Mavis and our confrontation and conversation, she was yielding. I was sure her intervention on Roy's behalf was motivated by the magnificent fact that he and I were chums.

'How do you figure that out?' asked Roy.

'Figure what?'

'That she took up for me.'

'I can't figure that at all. I guess you're right, Roy. Maybe she *is* crazy.'

'Of course she's crazy!'

The roast breadfruit was steaming hot and velvety good although, with a little piece of something in the way of meat or fish, it could have done better. But we ate our fill and I wondered just how I'd manage supper.

Roy Penner doused the fire and we broke camp and went our separate ways. I was sorry for him, knowing that come bedtime he'd have to kneel and reel off that *Pray Momma* stuff while I'd clasp my hands in earnest, talking with God about the fish-pot or praying a little something about Daphne.

CHAPTER 9

A bird as big as a Grade-A chicken

On that same night that Roy and I had spent the afternoon at his hut there occurred, about two or three o'clock in the morning, a most deadly thunderstorm. I woke to flicking lightning, bassooning thunder and pebble-hard rain drops, which all lasted about a full hour. There had been no visible indication in the afternoon that there'd be rain. Not to Roy and not to me either. The old Man was right. Rain in those parts invaded with the swiftness of a thief.

To me it meant nothing. Well, the goats were afield and getting a dousing to the skin all right but what could a little drumming do to goats? Nothing. Only make them stand with their hind legs up close to the fore ones, almost touching, their bodies arched and their heads bent. To my knowledge rain has never hurt a single goat since Christendom, and apart from this fleeting thought of their goaty discomfort I gave them no further consideration.

I was happy to hear rain playing drum music on the zinc roof. Rain at night held a special magic to me, magic which made me pull the covers tight over me and sleep like a baby.

That was what I did.

But next morning when I ran into Roy standing on the banks of the swollen copper-coloured river, his eyes riveted on the dancing, foaming, streaming water, his hands double deep in his pockets, it suddenly struck me that the two of us, he and I, shared a major tragedy. The fish-pot.

'It's washed away?' I asked, making it sound as a statement just as well.

'Sure! That cord couldn't hold it. No way.'

'But how can you be so sure?'

Turning to me without speaking, he took a piece of wet cord from his pocket. The remainder of the leash where it had snapped. I had forgotten about the leash.

With the pot washed away I knew that I was in trouble. There was now no way of catching fish with which to pay off rascally Teppy. Could be he would rat on me now. Maybe I'd have to think of another way out. Perhaps double the payment in birds to four. Maybe he'd accept that as a fair settlement until such times when I could come through with some fish. I'd do that: keep the idea active in my head.

'I'm sorry, Roy,' I said, 'about the fish-pot.'

'Thanks, old man. But it's no matter.'

His face was extremely sad, not because of his recent loss but with a sadness which seemed deeply rooted there, established bit by grievous bit, over the years. And there seemed to be so much depth in his eyes.

Finally, much like a philosopher he said, 'Easy come, easy go.'

'What d'you mean, Roy?'

'I stole it,' he said.

'*Stole* it? The fish-pot?'

He suffered me a look of utter pity as though I were the smaller of the two, the less mature.

'That's right. I stole it.'

'Ah well,' I said. Like a man.

But he bothered me. For the rest of the day Roy had me thinking about him. The Old Man was right. Angelic he looked but a devil he was underneath. A prankster going beyond pranks to meddle in deeper things. Thefts? I didn't

82

like that. He might involve me. And in his quiet world, apparently, all this was natural. All this was a part of his life. There was nothing wrong.

The loss of the fish-pot prompted me to take action. Teppy had to be appeased. If I could kill four birds maybe he'd accept them in lieu of the fish.

So that afternoon I went on my first solo shooting expedition.

I turned my direction to a grove of logwood trees where, Roy assured me, birds always congregated.

My two trousers pockets were like huge balls against my thighs, so full were they of gravel. My catapult was zingingly ready.

Roy was so right, too, bless his little bird-knowing heart, the woods literally swarmed with birds, large and small ones, hopping from tree to tree, singing or cooing or grooming their feathers.

Oh boy!

My first shot was aimed overhead at a bird which had perched and which, by its musical wing beat, seemed a pigeon. But I missed and its frightened flight gave the other birds, which I hadn't even seen, their cue to panic.

A torrid flutter of wings, and birds flying in seven different directions I guessed. If only I had been a better shot. If only I had bagged my bird. It would have fallen more or less quietly and the others would have remained, continuing their grooming and singing. Instead they had fled. But, wait a blazing minute! A big bird, bigger than the rest, a true lumberer on the wings, flying somewhat blindly. It settled, the wretch, blindly, too, as best as I could make out.

He was big all right and demanded special treatment. So with a larger-than-average gravel I loaded my catapult, stretching the rubber thrusts as far as I could.

I took careful aim.

Fired.

Whap!

A direct hit.

An explosion of feathers, swirling – the feathers – falling slowly. Something more substantial falling. The bird.

Whump!

Whoopee! Why not? My first bird and so danged big. You're some shot, I said to myself in congratulation. Pick up your game.

So I picked it up.

But always, when there are great moments, there comes creeping, that sure-as-rainstorm humiliation.

It was not an edible bird. Edible maybe but not usually eaten. The eyes were the first to deflate me. An abominable owl.

I looked up in despair and in vain for all the birds had, by now, disappeared. One entire flock had regrouped and could be seen winging their way across the valley to the distant, deep-blue mountains. I had had my chance but had botched it. I'd have to wait another day to get Teppy his two birds, and time was running out.

But what was I worrying for? Such a glorious idea leapt mountain-high into my head!

Why be choosy over Teppy?

Who was he, anyway, but a downright blackmailer, a low-down cur? Wasn't he an eater of alligator jowls and snake chops? Why not owl roast as well for that scamp? And what a joke at his expense! Wait till I told Roy about that. For I'd have to find a body to share this with. It was too big, much too big for a single boy. Yes, I'd tell Roy, tell him without giving away my secret – the reason for the blackmail.

Slinging my catapult around my neck, I plucked the feathers off the dear dead owl and with my knife snapped off its head and therefore its blinking identity. By gorrah, it looked like a grade-A chicken at that. Teppy would never know.

I ran the distance to his house.

Smoke poured from his outdoor lean-to kitchen. He was cooking.

'It's me, Teppy!' I hollered so he could hear me in the kitchen.

He came out blinking smoke from his eyes and running at the nose. In one hand he held a knife and in the other a yam which he had been peeling.

'Ah, it's you, boy. An' I see you got me a bird. Where's the other one?'

'This is a big one, Teppy. It's good as two. You know that.'

'Two it's got t'be, boy.'

'Come on.'

He held up two fingers. 'Two!'

'Oh no,' I said.

'Give me no lip, boy.'

'All right,' I said. 'I'll take this here chicken back and to-morrow bring you two o' the scrawniest birds I can lay hands on.'

I turned to go.

'Chicken?' he said. 'Stop there, boy.'

I stopped.

'You know you's a right smart business man. I think I'll take that chicken. I was only jokin'.'

'But it counts as two.'

'All right, all right. But where'd you get it?'

'Never mind that.'

He laughed. 'Stole it, eh? But it's none o' my business jus' the same. If you gone an' stole from Tate tha's your business. You's fadher'n' son. Give it 'ere, boy.'

85

I gave it to him.

'Prime meat,' I said. 'Grade-A chicken.'

'Aunha. A good two pounds. Yes, it can count as two. Def'nit'ly. An' I was jus' sorrowin' me 'eart out that I got nothin' to eat but salt cod again t'night. Boy, you's not only a God-sen' but a good bargain keeper. But, mark – not a word 'bout this chicken. Or else I got to rat on you.'

'Rat on me? What for?'

'You think I don' know you stole this chicken from Tate?' He laughed ugly teeth of yellow.

'Oh,' I said.

'Run along, boy,' he said. 'An' 'member, I got you deeper'n deeper. I got you by the screws. You now a gal chaser an' chicken thief. Now, go!'

I ran like mad and if there were any dust on the path my heels would have smoked up a storm. What a dupe!

When I told Roy Penner he flipped out of his usual serious mood and jumped in the air and whoopeed several times, landing only to roll over and over on the ground, cackling like a mongoose-threatened Mother Hen.

'Oh boy, that's the joke o' the year. You're smart all right. Boy, oh boy!'

I absorbed the compliments. 'You got to fool those adults,' I said.

'I bet he'll be the first to eat an owl around here.'

'Serves him right,' I said. 'He was saying he ate alligator jowls. Owl's roast's an improvement as far as I'm concerned.'

Roy laughed like mad. 'Boy, oh boy,' he said. 'Ahoo! Ahoo!'

But soon he resumed his seriousness and deeper ways and asked what I had been afraid he would want to know.

'What do you have to pay him for?'

But I was ready.

'Oh, he caught me at one of my pranks and decided to rat on me.'

'That's Teppy all over. What prank?'

'Smoking,' I said.

He grinned white rat's teeth. 'So you like it!'

'Oh yes. I'm a reg'lar puffer now. Thanks to you.'

'Oh, it's nothing.' Like any old philosopher. After a time he remarked: 'And he's still demanding a couple o' mountain crayfish per week?'

'That's right, the culprit.'

'I knew he was a bad egg, old man,' said Roy, 'but I didn't think he would go this far. He certainly romps rough.'

'He's a reg'lar highway thief.'

'Well, since I got you into this,' Roy said. 'The smoking bit I mean. I gather I can help you out.'

I jumped for that one. 'How?' I said like a drowning man hugging a straw. 'How, when you lost your fish-pot?'

'Oh, there's more than one way to skin a cat.'

'You're beautiful,' I said.

'Beautiful?'

'I didn't mean it that way,' I said.

'Oh, I'll show you tomorrow how.'

'And you won't tell tonight?'

'All right. You can catch them with your bare hands.'

'Your bare hands, Roy?'

Mountain crayfish have pincer-like claws, if not as large as those of lobsters, nearly so.

Roy read my thoughts.

'You get a little nip,' he said. 'But what's a little nip? It can be done. I've done it many a time, old man. You feel him out under his rock or between rocks and you take the first nip but in the end you can get him out of there.'

'Roy,' I said, 'you are a blessing disguised as a boy.'

'It's nothing,' he said.

'You're a trump. I mean it.'

'I like the bush and the river better'n going to school,' he said.

"Attaboy, Roy.'

'Thank you, old man.'

Slinging our arms over each other's shoulders, we walked home.

CHAPTER 10

Ahoo! Patoo!

Of course by the end of the week I looked nowhere as awful as I had done at the beginning. My hair was growing back. The ghastly brown of my scalp had given way to millions of tiny black hairs which had peeped through. And I was working like mad at the regrowth programme, pomading night and day, day and night.

Roy helped too.

He knew so many things which were useful. He gave me one of Mrs Jenkins's old stockings and after cutting the thigh end off we tied it, making a kind of skull cap out of it. Roy said it was good for pressing hair and conditioning it. Of course I had seen men wear them before. Those men who were thinking of attending a wedding or other function of equal importance. For twenty-four hours prior to their function they'd have their hair skull-capped and conditioned and prettily groomed. I didn't have much to be groomed but each night I pomaded my head and clamped on the stocking cap and woke in the mornings convinced that wonders had been wrought throughout the night, that my hair was a full millimetre longer.

Meanwhile, too, my stock was rising at school. Daphne and I were not yet on speaking terms but our war was off. George Kirby had definitely lost his sting. Daphne, it seemed, was avoiding him like a plague, apparently from the time I had embarrassed her with my little lie. He scowled at me, sure he scowled each and every time our eyes met, but he said not a bad word to or about me. Other boys had begun to act more friendly. The girls too. Shy but coming around. Only Marcia Donaldson, our fat girl, kept aloof. But she was not interested in any one. Only in candy. She ate a ton a day. Other students got punishment for misbehaving in class; Marcia was usually punished for eating candy out of turn. Yes, they were all coming around.

But something happened at school that threw me headlong into the middle of things.

Miss Clemens said the school was putting on a concert and our class *had* to do something. In the way of something she suggested, nay ordered, that we do a play. She had selected a play, she said and was ready to . . . Here she used a word which I think was audition. Anyway it amounted to our trying out the different roles to see who was best at them.

Among the characters were a king, his queen, a princess, a prince, a witch and a farmer. The king was fat; the queen a good wife; the princess beautiful; the prince (no relation to the family) handsome; the witch ugly and bad; the farmer a crusader.

If your guess is right, after the audition, Daphne had the witch's part and I the role of the protagonist farmer.

In that gossipy class of ours it caused quite a stir. That a couple of class enemies from warring families were going to play opposite each other was scandalous. Of course Daphne had to act a little as though the last thing in the world she'd like to do was act opposite me, saying: 'I don't want the part, I'm going to get out of the play,' and all that, but she was only acting. So soon. Girls all over and very Daphneish.

But Roy was shocked. Shocked, shocked, shocked! He seemed even sorry for me. But the shrimp lacked foresight. He couldn't see that our playing together was the ideal thing for breaking down the last barriers that stood between

Daphne and me. He didn't know that, in an inexplicable way, I liked Daphne.

All week-end, in every little spare time I could snatch, I mercilessly practised my part, speaking to the trunk of a banana tree instead of to the real witch, tearing at its dry leaves and pretending they were the witch's tresses.

Though I wouldn't hurt a hair of the real witch, **Daph**, Daph.

And oh, during that very week-end, I ran into her and it wasn't at church.

Among other things, Saturday in the country is firewood day. The Old Man who had gone to the nearest town to buy provisions and probably just to gad about as well, had told me to go to the woodlands and fetch a bundle of firewood.

Of course he knew I'd be in good hands, I'd be with Roy and that boy's cleverness and knowledge of the outdoors had reached the ears of even Dad.

Roy instructed me to pack some gravel shots and my catapult for, claimed he, the woodland literally choked with birds, flocks upon flocks of them. While we were there, he said, we could mix business with some bird-shooting pleasure.

The woodland was cool and damp and spongy under-foot and dark within, though in parts it was beautifully dappled by sunlight. There were so many trees and so many varieties of them. Trees for lumber and smaller broom-thatch palms, so many ferns. Hanging vines were there, vines that would please Tarzan to death.

There were birds all right – pigeons and baldpates, brown and ground doves, and even the beautiful-coated parrots and robin redbreasts, fleeing in flight as we thrashed through.

Firewood was everywhere too, provided mainly by yesteryean lumber men who had taken what they had required of a big tree, namely the trunk, and left the branches and twigs which were now tinder-dry.

Away we chopped with machetes, resting when our arms tired, and whenever we did we could always hear the echoes of other choppings of other boys cutting wood in other places.

Soon we had chopped enough for two and we bundled them with hog-meat strings which were simply vines.

Then Roy suggested a smoke and we lay on the damp ground, puffing away, jumping up only when we realized that the falling of berries all around us meant that the birds were feeding right above us.

We got ready for some honest-to-goodness shooting and, in his first shot, Roy got a dove.

I missed my first but since it was a pigeon which is considered a 'big' bird, I did not feel too badly.

Roy got himself a baldpate which was quite a prize and achievement, considering that the most outstanding trait of that bird is unadulterated wildness. It snaps off a branch at even the slightest shift of wind and you should see it fly in jerks. In constant panic.

Roy felt so exhilarated. 'Look at him, old man!'

'Yes, Roy. He's beautiful and you're a crack shot.'

Yes, I was beginning to feel real small, lamenting my uselessness with a catapult.

Roy said, 'What the heck? You shot an owl, didn't you?'

'That's nothing. An owl is practically blind in the days.'

'So what?'

'That's why I shot him, can't you see? He was helpless.'

'Oh.'

But I cheered up when, aiming carefully, I bagged a pigeon. It plunged like a dive-bomber into the undergrowth.

'See!' said Roy. 'See, old man!'

'Whoopee!'

'Bravo! As good a shot as any!'

It weighed about a pound and was fat.

Before we left the woods I shot another bird, a small one, a john-to-whit, and Roy bagged his third: a brown dove.

Satisfied, we started home, with our kill hanging on strings, and our firewood bundled and balanced on our heads.

But just before we emerged from the woodland whom should we run into? Thank you very much: Daphne Belmont.

She suddenly popped out of the thicket in front of us, a bundle of wood nicely balanced on her handkerchiefed head, walking crispy-missy as usual, as though she were on a paved road and on her way to church, swinging her hips and so her skirt.

Roy and I exchanged surprises with open mouths and enlarged eyes and I cleaned my throat but to no avail. Daphne continued on her crispy-missy way.

Where did she come from so suddenly?

Just then – ah me! She stumbled and tripped. Sprawling. The bundle of wood went flying and the vines that bound the faggots snapped. Wood scattered.

'Ouch!' from the darling girl.

'Boy!' from Roy.

'You see that?' from me.

Setting down my bundle of wood, I ran to her, raising her up. 'Are you hurt?'

But she pulled away from me without answering. Ungrateful wretch.

Glancing back I could see that Roy was still standing in the same place and I wished I had done the same sensible thing. As I gathered together Daphne's scattered firewood, he began to walk up. Something to do to blunt my rebuff. I got them all and once more encircled them in vines which

93

were stronger than the first. While I worked Daphne stole glances at me but as for words, she spoke nary one.

'There!' I said somewhat cheerfully when I was finished. 'Thank you, Beppo!'

I had never heard her enunciate like that before. It sounded very formal and like part of a speech or recitation.

By this Roy had caught up.

I winked at him saying: 'Help me lift this, Roy.'

He put his bundle down and between us we lifted Daphne's load back on to her head.

'Thank you, Beppo. And Roy.' With the same gunfire enunciation.

And she was gone. Nothing more said. No smile. No goodbye.

'She is crazy,' Roy said.

'Oh, I don't know about that. She's more ashamed than anything. Because she fell and we saw.'

'Did you see the fall?'

'Did I see it? Of course I saw it!' I said.

'I bet,' he propounded, 'that she did it on purpose.'

'On purpose? And risk skinning her knee? Why would she want to do a fool thing like that? Nonsense.'

But the more I thought about it, the more it looked odd, the way she had gone down, reluctantly yet not making a single effort to prevent the fall. Something stiff about it I mean.

'You don't know women,' Roy said. 'They're crazy. They like to do these things.'

'How'd you know what they like to do, Roy?'

'I know, old man, that's all. Look. I seen Miss Clemens drop her handkerchief on purpose just so she could see if Mr Ladd would pick it up.'

Mr Ladd was our principal.

'Yes?' I said. 'She did that? Our Miss Clemens?'

'Yes is right. She dropped it and he just about broke his danged neck going after that handkerchief, grabbing it up. And she . . . she smiled with so much superiority.'

'Are you sure it was superiority and not love, Roy?'

'She smiled and I didn't like the way she did it. It was both love and superiority.'

'So he loves her, that Mr Ladd!'

'Of course he does! Where are your eyes?'

'In my head.'

'Well, use them, old man. He's always looking at her. And how many times does he come in our class each day? I can't count the times. He times it right so they both walk to school in the mornings, too.'

'That's lovely,' I said. 'Real lovely.'

I was impressed by his powers of observation. If anything were going on between those two it had slipped by me.

'I bet he's going to marry her,' said Roy.

'Not a bad match, those two.'

'Same thing Daphne just done,' he continued. 'She tripped herself to see if you'd pick her up and her blinking wood.'

'Me? What makes you think she wasn't testing you?'

'I wasn't the one who broke his neck to pick them up,' said Roy. 'It was you.'

'I picked them up but didn't break my neck.'

'Lord, you bested Mr Ladd going after her and her stupid wood.'

'I had no special reason, Roy. You know that.'

'What beats me is why you stormed in so fast to do it.'

'It's the gentleman's way,' I said. 'As simple as that.'

'Gentleman's way, gentleman's way. Who you trying to fool? She made a slave of you. And you had the guts to ask me to help!'

'It was good manners to help,' I said.

'Good manners my granny! Women are crazy,' he said. 'And did you notice how hoity-toity she was? Did you realize she just about said Mr Beppo and Mr Roy? "Thank you, Beppo. And Roy." Son-of-a-gun!'

I guessed he was a woman-hater all right.

'She did. I must agree, Roy. But it was all shame that made her act so.'

He gave me another pitying look and had another poke at women-kind.

'They're all crazy. Daphne is crazy.'

We went home quietly, he glowering and I glowing.

The only untoward incident that marred the glorious week-end was how close I got to being thrashed by Teppy. It went like this.

Later that day, because it was the last day in the week, and I must pay up Teppy or be ratted upon, Roy decided he'd help me out in catching a few fish by hand. So we went to the river which by now was back from its flood state to its docile self. The water was no longer the colour of dirt. It was transparent and a nice blue too.

We took off our shirts and rolled up our shorts to the crotch and waded into a rock-filled pool.

Briefly Roy lectured me on how to poke my hand between or under the rocks where the fish remained in the days. Demonstrating, he shoved his arm, all the way to the pit, under a conglomerate-type rock.

Suddenly he pulled it back.

'There's one there all right.'

'Did its bite hurt?'

'Oh, it's just a nip.'

'Does a nip hurt?' I asked.

'It's nothing,' he assured me.

Once again his arm disappeared into the water and under

the rock. By watching his face work I knew what his hand was doing and how the fish was behaving as well.

Finally he said: 'Got him.'

And he did too.

A medium-sized grey mountain crayfish with tapering feelers and a small saw on the top of its head. In Roy's hand he flapped: *bap! bap! bap!*

Roy held him in such a way that the pincer-like claws were clamped together and therefore harmless.

'See, old man?' he said.

'Oh boy!' I said.

'Your turn,' he said, pocketing the fish.

With his arm he buzzed another rock. 'Here's one for you,' he announced as any professional teacher.

'For *me*?'

'Well how'll you learn, old man? You have to try.'

'That's true,' I said, taking a last look at my hand in its unnipped state.

'It's not hard,' he said. 'You push your hand under – easy, easy, easy like, and when you have the position of his claws . . .'

'And a nip,' I said.

'Ah, it's nothing. Once you know where his claws are you pin them down and nab him. But . . .'

'But what?'

'The claws aren't all, old man. Try to get them far up enough. Far up so you can hang on to its head or its feelers or moustache or whatever you like. For some of them'll part with them claws rather than come with you.'

'Oh well,' I said. 'Here goes.'

'Good luck.'

'Is he a big one?' I asked.

'About the size of this one.'

I inserted my arm just the way he had instructed me and

soon bumped into the pincers and, getting my little nip, pulled my arm back. But it was indeed a nip. No cut. No blood.

'See?' he said.

I returned my arm, and doing as he had said, tried to over-reach the pincers this time and – hallelujah! – I got him by the head and pulled the brat out.

He was about as big as Roy's and quite bappy too. *Bap! Bap! Bap!*

'See?' said Roy, I supposed happy at his teaching talents.

'You delight me,' I said. 'Why you use a fish-pot when you can catch them this easy, beats me.'

He had news for me.

'You can't always find rocks with fish under them,' he said.

'But this river has rocks everywhere,' I told him. 'Look.'

Truthfully they were all about.

'Sure, sure,' outdoorsman Roy said. 'But your arm's not always long enough to get at them fish.'

'Oh, I see what you mean.'

And he was right because although we tried the same pool for better than five minutes we didn't find another suitable fish refuge.

But we caught three others, he two, in other pools upstream.

I decided I'd hand over my catch to Teppy. Roy accompanied me and since, on paying up I'd have no fish left of my own, he promised me one of his.

'Thanks, old buddy,' I said.

He would hand it over as soon as I had returned from my business with Teppy.

But when we neared Teppy's home Roy stalled. This was as far as he'd go, he said.

Why, I asked.

'Cause Teppy was mean, he said.

And that I could understand. Teppy should be avoided by one and all. Perhaps on seeing Roy's fish he'd quickly devise a means of getting them too.

So Roy waited in the field of bananas which was close by.

'Here's your fish, Teppy!' I called.

He wasn't cooking today but was in the house somewhere. On hearing me he came out, faster than I'd expected. Maybe his taste for crayfish was mighty powerful. Or the food value of owl's meat was even more potent than alligator jowls.

'Bring 'em 'ere, boy.'

He stopped on the verandah.

I climbed the steps to join him and he took the fish but as he did so he grabbed hold of my wrist.

'You littl' rascally devil,' he said.

'What're you doin'?' I asked, quite alarmed.

'I goin' t't'rash you, tha's why.'

'You wouldn't dare! I'd tell Dad this one.'

'Oh yes? What kin' o' bird you made me eat, boy? Answer me!'

'Chicken!' I said.

'You lyin' rascal, you! 'Ow come if it was chicken, boy, your littl' frien', Roy, been actin' like an owl every time 'e sees me. 'Ow come this Roy been doin' that?'

'Which Roy?' I asked, stalling for time.

So that was why Roy had chosen to stay behind and not come into the yard! He knew what he had done, the little rat!

Teppy was angry all right.

'Boy, I don' like nobody makin' a fool out o' Teppy, y'ear!' He backed me up in the corner. The verandah rails were low enough for a boy my size to vault over but he was smarter than that. Where he had cornered me there grew a thick swath of climbing vine-like plants, the decorative ones.

There was little chance of my breaking through that almost solid net of vines and leaves.

He began to loosen his belt and, to tell the plain truth, I was not only sweating but marking time. I felt, too, that had I the choice I would have had a pee because during a thrashing it could very well happen.

'See here, Teppy,' I said. 'I don't know what you're talking about.'

'You'll soon know, you littl' rat. Every time I run into your frien', Roy, 'e makes fun o' me. Buckets o' fun. "Ahoo!" 'e says. "Patoo!" 'e calls.'

Here he put his thumbs into his ears and paddled his fingers.

'This 'ere's 'ow your frien' abuses me. "Ahoo! Patoo!" That's 'ow I know you feed me owl meat, boy. Tha's why I goin' t't'rash the daylights out o' you, boy.'

I wished Roy had tipped me off.

But I still had my head. Roy might be the prince of busybodies but I was still fast with my head.

The buzzing of bees came as a saviour. And there they were, bees a dozen strong, buzzing the small pink flowers of the decorative plant that climbed up Teppy's verandah. A little fib wouldn't hurt and it would save me from a beating too. I was a good actor.

'Teppy,' I said, my eyes big with alarm.

'What is it, boy? You got somethin' to say before I keel-haul you?'

'Quick! There's a bee on you!'

He jumped. 'Where, boy, where?'

'On your ear!'

He batted with a hand.

'Where's it, boy? Where's it?'

'On your neck now!'

How he jumped over the place, brushing and batting and

going nicely off-guard! The way was clear. I took my chance. I ran like the devil.

'You lyin', cheatin' rapscallion!' he cursed, raging mad, strapping the poor brainless verandah rails instead of me. He was so vexed he wheeled and stamped and tore at his ear.

'Bees on your ear, Teppy,' he said. 'Bee's on your neck. Same as 'ow 'e gave me owl meat an' say it's grade-A chicken. Boy, you's the devil in 'ell!'

Saved now, I thought I'd poke him before I departed.

'Wasn't the owl's meat better than alligator jowls?'

He came at me from the verandah but I drew back.

'Lord, boy, don' ever let me catch you, you 'ear?'

'So then the blackmail's off!'

'Off? Off? It's double on, boy. It's double on. You rapscalliony scum o' the eart'! You lyin', cheatin' . . . !'

'Well, how am I to deliver if you plan to beat me?'

'You deliver, that's all. If I catch you, your back pocket'll be blazin' good an' hard, that's all. But deliver. Leave 'em fish right 'ere on the verandah. An 'em birds too. An' no more foolin'. An' you know what? I want t'ree birds an' t'ree fish instead o' two. For damages. You 'ear me, boy?'

'Over my dead body, Teppy.'

'Over your keelhauled body you mean. You'll see. Upon me word, you'll see.'

Out-smarted and out-done in every way.

I found Roy wallowing in dirt so hard and cackling so cackily that he looked more like a worm than a boy.

'You rat!' I said. 'Why didn't you tell me?'

'And miss all the fun, old man? Oh, boy!'

'Why if I hadn't got out of that one?'

'With your head, old man?'

The little rat, he knew when to commend too.

But we did have a good laugh and, of course, I was doubly proud of my head.

CHAPTER 11

Women are crazy

The mango season had made its debut and a few trees were bringing in ripe mangoes. Little pink and yellow cheeks of ripe mangoes showed distinctly among the green of other mangoes and of foliage.

Most of the mangoes are eaten by people but animals too, especially cows, join the bandwagon. A cow will pick up a mango at every chance she gets – be the mango green or be it pink-ripe.

On that same Saturday evening, apparently, one of Mrs Belmont's cows displayed her blind love for mangoes by picking up one that was more green than ripe. Now when a mango is good and ripe, it's juicy by the powers and, on arriving in a cow's powerful mouth, the pulp squashes easily around the seed which is small enough for a cow to swallow, but when it's green or half so, it's an almost solid thing. And if it's a big one as this braggadocio cow had set itself the aim of ingesting, then there can be fireworks in the throat region.

There were fireworks!

The Belmont cow choked on the mango. It lodged securely in the throat.

As I later heard, the animal soon started to breathe with difficulty and to be puffed up in the belly parts and any amount of slimy stuff streamed from its nostrils.

The word flew around on wings and soon a gathering of people was at the Belmont's yard. At any rate, when I got there, there was a tidy crowd made up mainly of boys and men, surrounding the cow.

Mrs Belmont was busy fisting the animal in the back as a mother might burp a baby, but to no avail. The mango didn't budge and the cow's belly continued to balloon outwards and stuff dripped in long ropes from its nostrils and mouth.

It was my first adventure in the Belmont yard and a quick glance showed me that although the house was large it was ungainly. I mean it was built in a haphazard fashion. They must have started out with a small structure and built around it. A little piece one year and another room the next and so on until it was at the present stage. There was not much to it: a porch here, another around the corner, the roof tilted steeply here, and merely slanted in another place.

When Daphne saw me she eyed me with some surprise all right, but on seeing that in those starry eyes of hers was no trace of hostility, I sidled up to her.

'What a thing, eh?' I said.

'I'm so worried,' she said, glancing at me but, however, doling out the major part of her attention to the stricken animal. Stupid cow.

'That cow must be in severe pain,' I said.

'I bet,' she said. 'And she's so nice!'

'Think it will die?'

A pretty dark and daft thing to have asked but she replied without malice: 'I hope not.'

She was talking after all. Crises can remove mountains and shatter barriers.

'Would you cry if she dies?'

'Of course I would.'

'I hope she lives,' I said, finding it strange but rather cleansing for me to have said such a nice thing.

But I paid no further attention to her because, generally speaking, I'm more interested in crises that centre themselves around animals and vehicles than I am in girls. Even in Daphne.

The chatter was confusing. Everybody talked and none knew what he was talking about nor was anyone making any concrete suggestions as to how to relieve the animal. Until the clip-clop of a horse was heard and somebody said, 'Tate!' and turning, I saw the Old Man in the buggy.

'Tate's good wit' animals,' somebody else said.

'Come 'ere, Tate!' another shouted. 'Double quick, man! Cow's swallered a mango!'

He turned into the yard and jumped down from the buggy and, as soon as he had determined what was wrong he said, 'Martha' – speaking to Mrs Belmont, if you please – 'a bar of soap and a basin of water, Quick!'

As willowy as a girl, Mrs Belmont dashed into the house.

Meanwhile the Old Man began to unbutton and to roll up his sleeves. Everything of the doctor about him.

When Mrs Belmont returned with the prescription that he had ordered, he quickly began to rub the soap between his hands to the great puzzlement of all. But the magnificent thing about this, to me at any rate, was the fact that Mrs Belmont held the basin while he rubbed away. Once or twice he looked up and into her face and there was eye talk of some almighty sort but you couldn't make out anything in either face. It was good though. I thought as sure as anything that this would be the end of their stupid feud. Daphne and I had ended ours, so to speak, and I could see no sensible reason why these two weren't going to get on speaking terms as well.

But my daddy made a good many suds, meanwhile the cow was grunting low in her throat and wheezing.

The Old Man said, 'I'll be needing a bottle, Martha.'

And the tight-lipped woman relinquished the basin to a man and ran into the house to fetch it.

With everyone peeking to see, the Old Man poured the sudsy water into the bottle and approached the ailing cow.

'Give a hand here, Manuel,' he said.

Manuel, a short and stocky man, moved up to centre stage and, grabbing the animal by the horns, yanked the head up so that the Old Man could pour the stuff down the throat. Or more correctly into the throat since the mango was blocking that unfortunate passage.

But it wasn't long before the slippery stuff did its job.

Against the flood of liquid and no doubt the bad taste as well, the cow coughed and – *abracadabra*, and *bip*! – out of its mouth shot the green mango. And it was green all right.

'Bravo!' went the cheers.

'Hurray fo' Tate!'

Mrs Belmont was open-mouthed. Daphne, she laughed and clapped her hands and I, I winked at her.

But all that was nothing. In great relief the cow splatted some dung on the grass, an action which, under the terrible circumstances was understandable, quite understandable, but would you believe that it took a step forward and calmly set about to have another bash at that mango! Yes, sir. But my pappy kicked it out of the way and again the cheers went up.

With the excitement over, the men had begun to leave.

Mrs Belmont was very relieved but also very grave. 'How much do I owe you, Mr Tate?'

So formal.

'Nothin', Mrs Belmont. Not a farthing.'

Oh brother! While the wretched crisis lasted he had warmed up to her first name but now he was back to his formal self.

Daphne watched her mother's face.

'I'd like to pay.'

'Oh no,' said my Old Man. 'It's a community service. I'd do it for anybody. You know that as well as anyone.'

''Cause you see, I like to pay my way.'

The Old Man first walked away. He was annoyed too. No good at tramping, he was tramping now. He climbed aboard and on seeing me, he motioned to me and I joined him on the seat.

For a time we rode in silence and it was just as well for it gave me time to think about the recent incident.

Women! Like daughter, like mother! She was Daphne all over again or vice versa. The performance was so much like that of the daughter that morning in the woodland. 'Thank you very much, Beppo. And Roy.' And then she had traipsed away. They were getting on my nerves. Roy was right again. Women were indeed crazy. Crazy as hell – if Mrs Jenkins would please pardon the expression.

The buggy smelt nicely of fresh bread and peppermint candy and less nicely of staling meat and the Old Man's rummy breath but I didn't fault him for the breath part. I guessed when a man went out only once per week he was entitled to let himself go a bit and have a few grogs in the bargain.

When we reached home we unloaded the provisions and we backed the buggy into its house and unharnessed Boysie who had perspired two great wet patches on both sides. The Old Man shoved into my hand a white candy stick with a red line snaking attractively around it and I had an immediate go at it.

While he prepared dinner we talked of this and that.

'Do you ever think of getting married, Dad?'

'Why, Beppo?'

He was preparing fish for cooking.

'Well, I don't know, Dad. But it's not so nice to see a man cooking all the time. Wearing an apron and washing dishes.' He had an apron on.

'What's wrong with that?'

'Oh, I don't know for sure. Seems to me it's a woman's job.'

'I see. Getting tired of my cooking I suppose?'

'Oh no, sir. I like your cooking. You cook like a wonder.'

'Thank you.'

Although he smiled, I didn't like the fact that he had started thinking in terms of my dissatisfaction. Because I really wasn't dissatisfied. So I was glad when he shifted the conversation.

Had I got the firewood?

Yes, I had. Chopped and stored in the buttery.

Did I have any trouble?

None at all, Dad.

Were the animals looked after?

They were, they were: the calves penned separately from the cows, the goats brought home and bleating in the buggy house and the chickens fed a supper of diced coconuts and here now, Dad, I would attend to Boysie.

So I led the horse by the halter to the pasture, he doing a kind of sneeze between his teeth all the way down and even after he was let loose. Good old Boysie.

Dinner was good but not exactly terrific. It seemed to me that it lacked that special touch of the Old Man's. The fish tea was okay – peppery, well seasoned and salt-porky, but the flavour of the main dish seemed flat and the yam was definitely too salt.

The Old Man was off tonight, I said. Why?

Himself an avid eater, he was tonight pecking at his food like a bird. He who was usually in good humour and chatty, cajoling one with niceties upon niceties: 'Isn't it good,

Beppo?' 'What you think of this, Beppo, boy?' was silent tonight. Why? For what reason?

Chewing slowly, he seemed to be watching something on his plate, something imaginary. Definitely off tonight. Something bothered him.

I wondered if he had a problem which he was hiding from me. But what problem? He couldn't have been in debt! He had money which he lavished on clothes for me, upkeep for the place and on whopping good dinners.

The farm?

Maybe, maybe. But what? Crop failure?

He had a larger farm than the one we lived on, some twenty miles away, a farm forty acres or so large and planted with sugar canes. I hadn't yet been there but had been told it was a good farm, among the best, and had yielded a better-than-average crop. But maybe he had problems there. Mortgage problems. Or lease problems.

I wondered, too, if he gambled and on his sortie to town had played a hand or two of poker or dominoes or maybe billiards and had lost. I decided to find out what ailed the good man.

'Do you own all your lands, Dad?'

'What, Beppo? What do you mean?'

Dinner was finished, the dishes washed, the Old Man piping up a smoke and I was leafing through a war comic book.

'I wondered, sir, if you lease any of your lands or you own them outright.'

'What makes you ask?'

'Nothing, Dad. I just wondered, that's all.'

'I own them, Beps. Though I don't see what a boy wants t'know that for.'

'Gee, Dad. I'm only interested in you.'

Smiling, he squinted at me. We were silent for another ten minutes until I asked: 'Do you play games, Dad?'

'What kind of games?'

'Card games . . . Dominoes . . . You know? Billiards . . .'

'Dominoes.'

'For money, Dad?'

'No. But what the devil is this?'

He sounded irritable.

'Nothing, sir.'

He puffed away faster than ever and the shadow of the smoke on the wall was fascinating to watch. I let five minutes go by.

'Gee, Dad. I don't know. What d'you think of that Mrs Belmont?'

'What d'you mean, boy?' he snapped. Back from the faraway, lively as a hawk and almost as dangerous, styling me boy, his nostrils dilated. Uptight. So that was what upset him. Mrs Belmont. But I was cool. Was I ever cool! I'd have to go on as though I hadn't discovered anything.

'I mean, sir. The way she acted. You think she was mean?'

My words relaxed him, the devil.

'How did she act?'

'Wanting to pay you when you didn't help her cow for the money which was in it. Saying she likes to pay her stupid way. Stiff and prim-like.'

He shot to his feet.

'Stiff and prim-like! Saying she likes to pay her *stupid* way! Who taught you to speak in such terms of your elders, boy?'

Boy again. Fists clenched at his sides. Furious man.

'Sorry, sir.'

'Apart from the fact that Mrs Belmont and I don't see eye-to-eye, she's a swell woman, decent as they ever come and as proud as a bee!'

Stinging as one too.

'Yes, sir,' I said.

That was the greatest compliment I had ever heard paid Mrs Belmont and from her supposedly arch-enemy. Very confusing.

Without meaning to I said aloud: 'Roy must be right. Women are crazy.'

'What?'

'Nothing, sir.'

He had heard me all right. It was time to take a walk. I stood up and walked to the porch.

Here and there lights shimmered in the gathering darkness. Voices sounded and there was the occasional bark from a dog like a sniper firing a gun. The river was just a murmur.

At church the next day I met Roy. He looked almost smart now that he was dressed up in shoes and Sunday clothes, meaning long trousers, and wearing a jippi-jappa hat instead of a cap. Yes, his hands were deep in his pockets.

We swapped candies and I noticed that the one I got from him had been sucked before. It lacked the corrugated skin and was smooth. I gave him a piece of jackass corn, a thin, flat and tough cake which was among what the Old Man had brought home from the town.

'What d'you think, Roy? The Old Man fixed up Mrs Belmont's cow yesterday and she acted the same way as Daphne had.'

'What cow?'

So I told him.

'Jeez!' he said. 'A cow been so close to dying and I had to miss the stupid thing.'

His mind went far far away then it brought him back. He asked, 'How did she act?'

I told him that too.

'H'mm!' he said. 'Did you see Daphne?'

'Sure!'

'How'd she act?'

'Better,' I said.

'Did she say anything to you?'

'Yep.'

'What did she say?'

'I said something. I broke the ice.'

'What did you say, old man?'

'I asked her if she thought the cow'd die – know what I mean, Roy, buddy boy? And she didn't know.. I asked if she would cry – know what I mean? She said of course.'

'Jeez,' he said with some seriousness. 'I don't know, boy.'

'Don't know what?'

'You think they both love each other?' he asked.

'Dad and Mrs Belmont?'

'Sure. Them. Who the Samhill else?'

'I think so, you know. Strange things been going on. The Old Man was all upset afterwards. Barely ate his blinking dinner, and in the night I heard him cry out in his sleep.'

'Cry out?'

'Yes.'

'Nightmare?'

'He was dreaming all right. I asked him this morning. He said he was being choked. By man or woman I asked. He got mad.'

'It's crazy,' said Roy. 'People cutting each other's throat when they really love each other.'

'Sure, it's crazy.'

'It's true though. Love's a funny thing. There's always quarrelling and fighting.'

'It's stupid if you ask me,' I said.

Then he laughed the Roy Penner laugh.

'What now, Roy?' I asked.

'You never see a lane without a turning,' he said.

'What lane? What turning?'

'I'm wondering 'bout you and Daphne, old man.'

'You're crazy. Watch what fool thing you say.'

'Oh yes! Well, you two been busy cutting each other's throats, haven't you?'

'Not me. I told you we talked today.'

'Yes. And that's just the beginning. That's what you two were up to all the time.'

'Up to what?'

'Cutting throats to talk later and to love.'

'It's a lie,' I said.

But I liked every blessed word he was saying.

'I hate girls,' he said.

CHAPTER 12

A big coup

I had got myself into one or two things but it was Roy who got me into this one. Yes, sir, he did, the little chipper. There was no limit to the conspiracies of his little mind – bless his little mind just the same.

Almost everyone in our village has at least one mango tree in his yard. Teppy had one, Mrs Belmont, Mrs Jenkins two, and we also had one. But among some of the first that started to bring in ripe mangoes was Mrs Belmont's tree. They caught the eyes of many a child but just about as many who saw the fruits resisted the temptation and went his way.

On going back and forth to school I have to pass by this mango tree. It was lunchtime and I was heading back. Someone from the side of the road, where there was a clump of bush, said: 'Beppo.' Understand, in a whisper.

My investigation led to my finding Roy squatting in the bush. He signalled and I joined him and was dead quiet about it.

I had no real heart to venture on Belmont property for I had always remembered what Teppy had told me the first morning he had seen me – though he hadn't proved very reliable. Never to venture on that woman's property – for mango or for anything else, he had said. But Roy signalled me and I had joined him.

'What're you doing here?' I whispered.

'Bend down, old man,' he said.

I did as he had asked, my heart-beat tripling, and he confided in me that he was waiting for Daphne to head back to school and then we – the guts he had – he and I, could steal into the mango tree and take a few ripe ones.

'But she'll catch us, Roy.'

'She doesn't hear too good,' he said.

'Is she deaf or something?'

'I suppose so,' he said.

Just like that, and only that, he supposed so. What a boy! I didn't know which was worse, he or Teppy.

We hunkered down in the bush and I could hear ever so distinctly my heart beating pit-a-pat-pat. We didn't have to wait long before Daphne emerged from the house, singing a ditty and with a hog-meat string, skipping her way gaily to school. She passed very close to us but we were well hidden and she wasn't looking for intruders.

'Now,' said Roy. 'But you wait here.'

He must have read my fear of going into the tree. I was mighty happy to wait. I didn't want to be caught in the branches. On the ground, I thought, I'd stand a chance. I didn't like this adventure one bit because, if caught, the Old Man would be sore as hell – Mrs Jenkins, please pardon me again. But Roy, in his own quiet and mysterious way, had zapped his influence at me and won.

In tree-climbing that boy was like a monkey. Maybe better. Before I could have said Jack Robinson he had shinnied up that tree and, swinging from limb to limb, began to fill his pockets with mangoes. Plummies they were called and no bigger than plums were they. He could ram no fewer than a dozen of them in his pockets. And was he packing them in.

So absorbed was I in his cunning and agility that I never once took my eyes off him. Imagine my surprise, then, when someone tapped me on the shoulder, saying: 'Aha!'

You guessed correctly: Mrs Belmont. She was almost on top of me and terrifyingly tall.

'Stand up!'

I stood up and I trembled.

If what they said of her was true, and if her hate of the Old Man were genuine and extended to me, then I was going to have it. To the police with me? Court? And then jail?

I wasted no time in pleading my case.

'I didn't mean to, ma'am. It's not me, ma'am. It's the boy in the tree.'

'Heh!' very cruelly. 'You there in the tree,' she called. 'Come on down here, you little monkey.'

I concluded that this woman could very well be a sadist of some kind. She was going to do something to us, and she was going to enjoy herself.

'You little rats,' she went on. 'You bare-faced rats.'

Her voice was semi-masculine, rasping a bit but rich and tuneful.

Roy began to climb down. I had never seen anyone as frightened as Roy and to think that he was the gutsy one, the brains behind it. I say he looked the more frightened because, of course, I couldn't see myself to determine the extent of my fright. But he, his eyes were as bulbous as eggs and he shook like anything. He had also wet his pants. Real weak bladder he had.

'Do you know what happens to mango thieves?' Mrs Belmont asked.

'Yes, ma'am,' said Roy now down on the ground and still trembling. He sought an opportunity to bolt but our captor wasn't taking chances: she held us by our wrists. Yes, sir.

'I was only waiting for him,' I said.

'Oh yes? In the bush? Big joke.'

'He asked me to, ma'am. It's you, Roy,' I accused him. 'You're responsible. It was your idea.'

Mrs Belmont wasn't hardly listening. 'What's your name?' she asked.

'Beppo, ma'am.'

'Beppo what?'

'Beppo Tate, ma'am.'

'Hah! So you're the one!'

'The one what, ma'am?'

She didn't answer. She looked at Roy. 'You,' she said. 'How many years you been stealing my mangoes?'

Roy kept a buttoned mouth.

'Answer me, boy!'

'I won't do it again, ma'am.'

'Unload your pockets.'

He did it and with so much speed.

'Wet your pants, eh?' she observed. 'Well, that's punishment enough, my man.'

'Yes, ma'am.'

'Run along.'

He scooted. Boy, did he scoot! The path was a beaten one and his bare feet flagged it with a sound akin to a whip's lash. He didn't look back once. As far as he was concerned we weren't friends, he hadn't got us into this, and I hadn't been left behind holding the bag, so to speak. From now on, I thought, I'd have to watch that boy. He had got me in deep waters with Teppy. And now this. I'd have to be careful of keeping company with him. He had made me accessory to this theft and had – lucky brat – left me in the mess.

'What about me, ma'am?' I began to sniff, hoping to God it was one of my best productions.

'Up to the house with you,' she said.

'What for, ma'am?'

'Go on! Your impertinence asking questions.'

'Yes, ma'am.'

She didn't let go of my wrist at all and she made me enter

the house in front of her and at a single glance – though I had little interest in such things – I saw that the place was as clean as a whistle and the chairs and tables of a wood such as mahogany and well polished too. The centre table was covered by a white enbroidered tablecloth and held a vase of sweet-smelling flowers, prettily arranged. Perhaps – the flowers – a handiwork of Daphne's. But all in all a nicely-kept house.

'Sit down.'

I sat. I was more scared now than before. What was she up to? I didn't feel good. Did she mean to keep me here then send for the Old Man? People were right. She and my Old Man were true-born and unrepentant enemies. See, she had released Roy, the instigator of the theft and the real thief. Me she had held. No fair, no fair.

'Where are you from?'

We were seated face to face, eye-ball to eye-ball. She had nice eye-balls.

'Santa Cruz, ma'am. That's in St Elizabeth,' I added as relish.

She had a straight nose and fine mouth and a chin so firm. A hair or two protruded, curled, from the firm chin and as they say, a woman with a single hair springing from her chin, where the presence of hair is the mark of a man, is strong. She was strong, strong as a lion. Or lioness. Her eyes were okay too but I couldn't make head or tail of them. Now they were hateful, now loving as a puppy's; once mocking, another time sympathetic.

'What kind of parents you have, boy?'

'Fine, ma'am. But poor.'

'They must be very poor to give you away to Tate. Hah!'

'He's very . . .' There was no point in antagonizing the woman any further.

'He's very what?'

'Oh nothing, ma'am.'

'Go on. You want to go back to school, don't you?'

'Yes, ma'am.'

She looked sideways and, following her eyes, I saw an alarm-sized clock on a shelf. Ten minutes to one. At one precisely the bell would go. Nearly a quarter-mile to school. Ten minutes to get there – if I were released in time or released at all. Funny thing though: I hadn't heard the clock before, but now that I had seen it, I declare it ticked as loudly as a grandfather's clock, only faster.

'He's very what?'

'Well, he's not very anything, ma'am. But he's okay I guess.'

'He?'

'Well, he's not too bad a man, ma'am.'

'He's not worth two pence as far as I am concerned, young man. He makes my stomach *sick*.'

And yet·she didn't look anywhere like a sick stomach. She even seemed to like saying the things she was saying: jibing the Old Man but not meaning a single thing she was saying.

'Does he feed you well?'

'Oh boy! Does he?'

'Work you hard?'

'No, ma'am. Not at all. That man lets me lead a charmed life.'

'See? Stupid!'

'Who, ma'am?'

'Tate of course. A boy like you needs plenty of horse-type work to keep you out of mischief.'

'You don't mean that, ma'am.'

'Of course I mean it. Or why are you in this?'

'I told you, ma'am. It was the other boy. I was just waiting for him. Holding the bag, so to speak. May I go now, ma'am?'

'Do you like milk?'

'Oh yes, ma'am. Do I like milk! I drink three glasses a day.'

She got up.

Seven blinking minutes to one.

Miss Clemens had a funny way about her, a way of detaining people thirty minutes for being late two.

'May I go please, ma'am?'

Without answering me she went into the next room and I could hear stuff being poured and when she emerged again she was carrying a glass of milk.

'Here.'

'For me, ma'am?'

This was madness at a high rating.

But I took it.

'Drink every drop of it,' she ordered, rolling the 'r' in the last syllable of every.

To my horrors I found that atop the milk floated a scum of thick cream, something I hated massively.

'But the cream, ma'am.'

'It's good for you. Drink up.'

'Yes, ma'am.'

Daphne would have been just as bossy.

Even though I could have screamed when that rag-like cream slurped into my mouth – yech – I had to drink it.

Six minutes to one.

'I suppose you'll tell Tate about the mangoes?'

Tate again. Just two days before, on Saturday, she was styling him Mr Tate.

'No, ma'am. I won't ever tell him about the mangoes.'

'Why not?'

'He'd strap me, Mrs Belmont.'

'Good.'

The sadist in her.

'And our little talk?'

'I won't tell him that either, ma'am.'

'Run along then. And I hope you get the strap for being late.'

Yet she said it, I think, without having meant it. I would have scooted just as Roy had but she said:

'One other thing.'

'Yes, Mrs Belmont, ma'am?'

'Do you know Daphne?'

'Yes, ma'am. Do I know her! Boy!'

'What's so special?'

'Oh nothing, Mrs Belmont.'

'You're in the same class?'

Something she already knew.

I told her we were indeed in the same class.

'Well, if you ever lay hands on her, I'll skin you.'

'I know, ma'am.'

'You know what?'

Couldn't make her know my opinion of her so I said: 'I know I mustn't lay hands on her, Mrs Belmont.'

'Good. Since you know that.'

Five minutes!

'And your Mr Tate as well. I'd like to skin that man Hah!'

'May I go please, Mrs Belmont?'

'One more thing,' she said with the faintest trace of a smile. 'If you don't tell Daphne about this, I won't tell her either.'

'Thanks, ma'am. Thank you very much. For everything. For your mercies and milk.' I showered everything on that pretty-puss lady and she smiled a wee bit, snapping: 'Go!'

And did I ever go! Did I ever burn up that turf! Did I?

When I hit the school yard the bell had stopped ringing but I managed to get in with the tail end of my class.

So convinced was he that I had been whipped that Roy had a hard time keeping himself from laughing at me. But I wasn't furious at him. I was more confused than anything.

Mrs Belmont sure was a strange one. Instead of whipping the accessory to a theft she had quenched his thirst with milk and lightened his load with talk. Yes, she was strange. This bit of taking me up to the house and talking to me about every blessed thing except the misconduct, then giving me something to drink, was the strangest reaction to theft I had ever heard about. And her references to the Old Man. A lot of bad things honeyed over with a nice tone of voice and little bursts of *Hah!* And I should keep it from Daphne.

Wait till I told Roy that one. I'd even add a few things as well to make him suffer.

And at recess time, Roy was at my side, whipper-snapping happy over his coup.

'What happened, old man? She beat the heck out of you, eh?'

'No,' I said with major nonchalance.

He wiped his silly grin off his face mighty fast.

'Then what happened, old man?'

'Oh nothing. We had a man-to-woman talk, that's all.' I slapped at a fly that was bothering me and said: 'Get!'

'What?' Roy said. 'A talk?'

Poor fellow.

'A man-to-woman talk!' he went on. 'I don't get it.' He was almost wild with confusion. 'Talk about what?'

'This and that. The weather. My family back in Santa Cruz. School life. Home life. A little nix, a bit of nox. Such things.'

'I don't believe it.'

'Have it your way then.' I turned aside. The rat.

Having thought that at least I had got a beating he had prepared himself for his usual Roy Penner cackle but I had news for him.

'We even had a little something for the belly,' I said, 'and for good measure as well.'

'Liar!'

'Okay.'

'What something?'

'Milk, Roy. A glass this tall.' I indicated one as tall as twelve inches.

'Milk?' he said with wide eyes.

'And pancakes.' I added this to make the pill a lot more bitter.

'Pancakes?' His face fell and it couldn't have fallen much more than it was in its natural state. Rodents have a fallen type of face anyway.

'Remember you telling me I was smart?'

'Yes,' he said hungrily.

'Well today was the day to prove it, Roy, sonny boy. I had Mrs Belmont eating out of my hands.'

'Jeez.'

'I can visit anytime I please. *If I please*. But I don't think I will. Wouldn't want the Old Man to feel upstaged, you know.'

'Boy,' he said. 'I wish I was the one who got kept.'

Poor boy. He was dazed all right. With his hands deep in his pockets he was walking away to lick his wounds when Jody Ramsy, two grades below us and a tyke for whom Roy had a soft spot, ran up and fondly jumped on his back. Roy flattened him to the ground.

'Vanish!' he said.

Little Jody didn't cry. He merely brushed red dust out of his clothes and came over to ask me. 'What's the matter with him anyway?'

'Oh,' I said. 'A little down in the mouth, Jody.'

'Oh?'

'And in the belly too, I guess.'

'What are you talking about?'

'Roy,' I said. 'Run along, sonny boy.'

CHAPTER 13

Rendezvous

Full two weeks went by and Teppy did not drop in at our place. In fact the Old Man hadn't seen him in all that time. Teppy missed having Sunday breakfast two weeks in a row and the Old Man said it was a phenomenon. He began to worry that Teppy might even be sick. For it wasn't like old Teps to pass up Sunday fare for two consecutive weeks.

'No, Dad,' I told him, 'he isn't sick.'

'How'd you know, Beppo?'

'I saw him, sir.'

And I had seen him, too. Was I seeing him? Twice per week. Once to deliver his fish and another his birds. Since the day he had threatened to beat the skin off me we had not met at close range because I wasn't all that careless. I picked up the habit of putting the delivery on the verandah then calling his attention to them. He'd come out and, if they were fish, he'd take them pronto into the kitchen but if they were birds, they underwent examination even though it was evident they weren't owls for I left them in feathers and with their heads on. With birds he didn't trust me. But whether he stayed to make his examination or plunged immediately back into the building I got in at least one tease.

'Ahoo! Patoo!'

Either he was too angry to respond or was acting on the principle that if ignored a nickname would go sour.

'Where'd you see him?' the Old Man asked.

'Oh, here and there. In the square. Near his house.'

'He must be vexed with me.'

'I don't think so, sir. I think somebody gave him a nick-name and maybe he's afraid to come around.'

'What nickname?'

'Ahoo, sir.'

'Ahoo?'

'Owl's cry, sir.'

The Old Man rocked his head and smiled. 'What for? Who'd give him a fool name like that?'

'Oh, I don't know, sir. But I've heard of the name.'

'But why? Teppy's not handsome by a very long stretch but he doesn't look any like a wretched owl to me.'

I didn't enlighten him further.

My being in the school play further enhanced my growing social life. You can't be in a play with people and not have some kind of communication with them.

As soon as rehearsals had begun I was talking with all the actors, laughing with them, helping them or they me. I was playing opposite Daphne and we laughed at the funny parts and touched one another and if that's not breaking the ice and keeping it broken I don't know what else is. So soon we were speaking in other situations as well. In class. On the red-earthed playground. On the road.

George, too, who was not in the play, had buried the old hatchet. We weren't great pals but he spoke to me and I to him. Sometimes. One day he even brought back my book from the desk of Miss Clemens.

'Thank you, George.'

'You is welcome,' he said.

Not good grammar but – God forgives – the brute was speaking.

They even got me to play the mongoose-and-chicken game.

Chicks, chicks, chicks!
We don't want your corn.

All of us, except Roy, lined up behind Daphne the sure-as-sunshine Mother Hen, defying the wiles of Mongoose, good old ex-bully George.

Chicks, chicks, chicks!
We don't want your corn.
What fat, fat chicks!
We don't want your corn.
But I must have a chick!
We don't want your corn.

After the first game Roy pulled me aside.

'How come you play in that game?'

'I was asked,' I said, looking anywhere but at him.

'But you said it was a sissy game, old man!'

'It's different, Roy.'

He hissed in his teeth. 'Different how?'

'Well we're in this play together – know what I mean? The prince and witch stuff. And things have changed a bit. Know what I mean? 'Cause, you see, this way we're getting good practice in acting. And it's good team spirit. See what I mean?'

Again he hissed in his teeth. 'I don't know about practice and team spirit and all the rest of nonsense. But I know I don't understand you,' he said.

'Aw, come on, Roy. Be a sport.'

He didn't care to be a sport just then but sauntered off with his hands deep in his pockets.

Anyway, with all that Roy was thinking about me, how I was such a so-and-so, I believe that Miss Clemens couldn't have done a better project than this school play. Because it had got me swinging with the rest of the class. And, of course, my hair had regrown. It was more handsome too than before. Isn't it always like that? If you scrape off your hair it will grow back more uniformly and more handsome, by george!

Everything was turning out great. Daphne, of course, bothered me slightly. She was too bossy. Anyway I decided I'd play along and as soon as I knew her better, put the old foot down.

Not since our confrontation that morning because of the goat, did we meet again at the farm level, but I had the strangest feeling that I was being watched. Her eyes bored into me. From behind some bush. From the ditch. Or from behind the safety of a rock in the river bed.

But we were doing fine, especially at school. Yes, we were.

One day, just as a way of opening a conversation I said, 'Daphne, what did you mean that morning when you pointedly said we – the old Man and I – didn't know what went on on our farm?'

'You mean you don't know that yet?' she asked with big white eyes.

'Know what?'

'How dumb!' she said with her usual superiority, turning away.

'Wait,' I said.

She waited, back turned to me.

'What's it we're supposed to know?' I asked.

'And you're so smart,' she said, turning to me and looking me up and down.

'What has it go to do with?'

'One thing first. What business do you have with Teppy?'

'I can't tell you that!'

'Oh? Then I can't tell you what you want to know.'

'How'd you know about me and Teppy?'

''Cause I'm smart. I keep my eyes open.'

What did I say? She was always watching from behind bushes. Or rocks. Or maybe ditches.

'I see. About Teppy. I just go visiting. We're pals. Isn't he a nice man?' I said and grinned.

'Nice? Visiting? Pals? Come off it. When he was going to beat the hide off you the other day?'

She knew everything.

'Boy,' I said. 'You seem to know everything.'

'Of course I do.'

'Roy told you about that. The beating,' I said as a matter of probing.

'No, he didn't.'

'Oh,' I said. She was something else. 'All right then. I sell him a few fish and birds.'

'Hah!' she said. I had heard that *Hah* before. Like mother, like daughter.

'I know about the birds and the fish,' she went on. 'But you don't sell them. How much for?'

'For . . . for . . . Look, Daphne. That's personal. You can't make me tell.'

'Hah! Hah! Hah!' Very dryly. 'And you can't make me tell either. You think I don't know Teppy? Such a dishonest man! You think he'd buy fish and birds from you when he could get them free!'

She knew Teppy. Everybody knew Teppy. A known rascal. Then why hadn't the Old Man warned me? Too good-hearted, I guessed.

But this Daphne, what a bargain she drove! If and when she got married this girl was going to wear the pants. She was curious but I was far more curious. I'd have to give a little.

'All right,' I said. 'Can you keep a secret?'

'Sure, I can. What you think I'm keeping from you now?'

'Okay,' I whispered. 'He's blackmailing me.'

'Blackmail! But that's bad! That fiend!' she snapped. She was on my side.

'Now it's your turn to tell me what you know.'

'What's he blackmailing you for?'

'That's not fair, Daphne. You promised to tell . . .'

'After you tell everything. Why does he blackmail you?'

I told her the same fib I had told Roy: that Teppy had caught me smoking. No point in telling her that my flipping curiosity about her name had trapped me. Fireworks that.

'You smoke?' she snorted with genuine alarm.

'Well . . .'

'You ought to be ashamed, Beppo Tate!' Top-quality scolding attitude, Mother Hen's stance. 'I don't like boys who smoke.'

'Wait a minute. It was only paper, Daphne.'

'It doesn't matter. Imagine you smoking! So young! So small!' Just like a little woman.

'What about your secret?' I asked.

'I'm so mad at you,' she said, fuming. 'I have a mind telling Miss Clemens about you.'

'You wouldn't.'

'Want to bet?'

'No, I don't want to bet. Besides you promised you'd keep it a secret.'

'Mannish,' she said. 'Brat! Show-off! Crazy fool!'

'And your secret?' I persisted.

'You'll have to wait.'

'But you promised!'

'You promised, you promised, you promised! Just like a baby! You really want to know?'

I spread my arms. 'What d'you think I'm pleading for all this while, Daph?'

My abbreviation of her name seemed to have pleased her. Somewhat anyway. She softened.

'Do you know where that big pear tree is?'

'The avocado? Of course! The one on our land?'

'Yes.'

'Of course. Shoot.'

'Meet me there at six in the morning,' she said.

'Are you crazy or something?'

'You want to know, don't you?'

'Meet you there at six. Oh brother!'

'That's right,' she said.

'In the morning?'

'In the morning,' she said, cool as a cucumber.

'But that's devil early. We don't usually wake up before seven!'

'Just be there, Beppo Tate.'

And she was gone. A Napoleon of a girl.

CHAPTER 14

Caught you!

To tell the plain truth I didn't sleep well that night. As a matter of fact, from the moment Daphne had pickled my curiosity, I didn't do anything well.

Being a lover of mangoes I had always eaten no fewer than six of them between school and supper time. That day I gathered them all right but wasn't hungry. Something was in my throat preventing me from swallowing. I bit into each and every one then threw it away, uneaten. Supper, too, went largely uneaten. I ate some, mark you, as much only to hide my state of mind from the Old Man.

In an effort to predict what lay at the bottom of this I sorely stretched my imagination all night. But I made no headway. I only knew it must be more serious than I had previously thought. I had no idea what it might be and I cursed Daphne, to high heaven, for stirring me up as she had.

Sleep? No, sir. I had no more than ten winks and they were very indefinite winks too. I spent the better part of the night counting the crowing of cocks and looking through the window for the first light of dawn, hoping to discover what?

As soon as the blur of trees became more distinct and the hazy outline of the mountains turned to a rigid cockscomb, I knew the dawn was there.

I eased out of bed, hoping to make as little noise as possible, but how that treacherous bed creaked as though it needed to be oiled.

But I managed to dress without making a single sound.

However, when I tried to open the back door, that was another matter. In all the times I had tried to open it, it had behaved as a perfectly trustworthy and co-operative door, with no squeaking whatever, but that morning it was different. It turned rebel. It creaked and wheezed a dozen hungry puppy noises and once the Old Man turned over in his bed. I froze. But he soon began to snore again. Thus reassured I entered the outdoors and scooted.

It was good scooting grass too, double wet with silvery dew which gave me one of the nicest foot-baths ever, before I turned on the path and pounded along it.

The path led to the river beside which stood the avocado tree that Daphne had mentioned. There I was to meet her.

She was there, standing on the sand in the river bed. Like mine her feet were wet. She was wearing a scarf tied beneath the throat. I swear she looked the regular dairy maid. Or shepherdess. Unspoilt and sweet. Sweet Daphne.

'Hi,' I said. 'Am I glad to see you? Now the mystery will be cleared up.'

She motioned me to follow her and we went upstream apiece then she climbed out on the bank, I following her, and she stopped behind a clump of bush.

'We wait here,' she said.

'*Here?*'

'Be quiet.'

'What's this all about?'

'Shhh!' she said, putting a finger to her lips.

I couldn't figure why we had stopped here. Or why we should remain hidden behind a stupid clump of stupid bush. What was here to discover? It seemed awfully like rubbish to me. All I could see were our cows and they only reminded me that should I stay here too long, fooling around, the Old Man would wake and, finding me gone, heaven knew where, get intolerably and early-morning mad.

Then somebody was coming. I could hear the swish-swish of feet and smell tobacco.

Teppy.

Daphne rolled her bright baby-white eyes at me. That I took to mean that I should be double quiet and squat and, as soon as I associated Teppy's appearance with the extra precautions, I had it. This whole mystery revolved around this prince of sneaks. He was carrying a pail and looking around in the most suspicious of manners.

He went directly to Mabel, the cow that I was responsible for milking, the very one whose milk supply had suddenly and inexplicably faltered.

Got it?

With the utmost disrespect, he kicked Mabel to her feet and without the slightest hesitation, squatted and began to milk away.

Daphne looked at me and smiled. 'See now?'

'I never thought . . . My granny! The culprit! Black-mailer! Thief! We couldn't figure out why her milk supply had dropped. Thank you, Daphne. Thank you so much.'

'What're you going to do?' she whispered.

'Nab him.'

'And then what?'

'I don't know. I'll play it by ear I guess.'

'Well,' she said with unusual humanity, 'he can't black-mail you any more.'

'So true! Thank you, dearest Daphne.'

'What? Don't you dearest me!'

There was no time to dispute trivialities even if they fell under the hallowed ground of romance, so I stepped from behind the bush and cleaned my throat.

Teppy wheeled so fast it was as though he were operated

by switch and on a cog, and so frightened the poor cow that the animal kicked a mighty foot into the grass. But Teppy jumped out of harm's way.

'Caught you,' I said with great police know-how.

'What you doin' 'ere, boy?'

'Catching you stealing my Dad's milk. That's what.'

For a moment he was tongue-tied.

'Boy,' he finally said, showing some fangs yet not laughing. 'You don' stan' a dog's chance provin' that. You's in enough trouble wit' me an' if you jus' as much as open your mout' I'll make you out as the worl's bigges' liar. You think Tate'll believe you? I got the screws on you, boy. I goin' home now an' you better make sure you keep your mout' shut. I'm not a good man. Everybody roun' 'ere knows. I'll make it bad for you, boy. You ever 'ear o' obeah? Tha's black magic, boy. I'll set g'osts on you. Nine days after you's good an' dead. You want to die or you want to live? Well, heed me, boy. Keep your mout' double shut. You didn' see nothin'. I be seein' you, boy.' He was turning away. He was a bad man all right.

'Stop!' I said. I was even smiling. But coldly.

He turned.

'All right, boy, you askin' for it. I'll even make it rougher for you. I'll go right to Tate an' tell 'im 'ow you been gettin' up in the night an' milkin' this 'ere cow an' givin' the milk to that girl Daphne. 'Ow 'bout that, boy?'

'Daphne,' I called.

She stepped from behind the bush as mad as seven devils. 'So you would, would you?'

When he saw her he almost collapsed. His eyes went big and bright and his mouth fell open and he was very uncomfortable.

'See, I have a witness, Teppy. You're caught, my man. And I'm not afraid of your ghosts and such nonsense. Man, you're wicked. You would tell the Old Man that I was giving the milk to Daphne, huh? Come back here.'

I pointed out a spot near my feet.

Slowly he started to approach.

'Come on!' I snapped. 'Step on it!'

He jogged the rest of the way.

And to see him jog.

'Now, hear this, Teppy. You're so mean I ought to get the Old Man to call in the police.'

'No, boy. Please no.'

'He's so good to you and this is how you repay him . . .'

'Please.'

'First you blackmail his son, then you turn around and take some of his milk and with the aim of trying to discredit me. And the cow as well.'

'I been takin' less now. Since that mornin' that Tate complained.'

'Yes, I notice that. She's gone up one quart to three. But it's not good enough.'

'Forget the birds and the fish, boy. No more blackmail. You free now.'

'That I know, Tepps. And no thanks to you.' I turned to Daphne. 'What shall we do with him?'

'The rat,' she said. 'Imagine what he said about me. Teppy, you're a diehard criminal.'

'Ah, Missy Belmont,' he said. 'You angel. Don' dirty your sweetness wit' condemnin' me. Talk to 'im. Talk to this littl' angel boy an' make 'im let me go. I'll be beholdin' to you.'

'You were so cruel to blackmail him,' she said coldly.

'I was awful cruel, Missy. But plead for me.' Afraid that the Old Man might be coming, he was looking behind him now.

Daphne said, 'I'll agree that smoking is bad for him and he

shouldn't do such a silly thing but you didn't have to black-mail him for that!'

'Blackmail for smokin', ma'am,' he said to Daphne, obviously seeing the opening. 'It was no smokin', Missy. This boy come right up to me 'ouse an' demand to know your name. Tha's what . . .'

'What?' said Daphne, looking from him to me with a face so surprised it emulated Teppy's when he had been caught in the act. 'And you told me it was smoking,' she said.

'Teppy,' I said. 'You're an utter fool. A jackass! I should get you arrested.'

'No, please no.'

'All right, Teppy,' Daphne said, looking somewhat pleased. Maybe the new information made her happy. The thing about her name. 'You can go now,' she said to him. 'We'll think of a suitable punishment,' she said to me.

'Thank you, ma'am,' he said, bowing down to her. 'A thousan' thanks to you littl' angel girl.'

And he was gone.

'What do you mean sending him away?' I accused her. 'Whose business is this anyway? And *we* will think of a suitable punishment! Doggone!'

'Well, didn't I play a part?'

'Sure, you played a part. But you didn't have to grab leadership and issue orders without me. Whom do you think wears the pants around here anyway?'

If I ever lived to marry that girl I would have a constant struggle to retain the pants.

'I shouldn't have interfered,' she said. 'I should've let him go on milking away. But next time.'

'I didn't mean it that way. You know that.'

'What did you want to know my name for anyway?'

'To find out if it was a stupid name,' I lied.

I had the feeling she knew I was lying.

'I see,' she said, 'and is it stupid?'

'Not really.'

'Well, I'll have you know it's a hundred times better than Beppo.'

I laughed and said recklessly, 'What's a name? How'd you know about Teppy?'

'Remember that morning when I caught your goat?'

'Remember it! Of course I remember it! My goat you kept prisoner and Teppy you let go. Twisted justice.'

'Well, I was out here real early that morning and I caught him doing it.'

'Why didn't you tell me?' I asked.

'I'm not supposed to be talking to you.'

'Why?'

'Adults are stupid, don't you know? Oops!' She covered her mouth.

'Don't be sorry,' I said, super-happy with this early-morning camaraderie. 'They're very stupid anyway. I didn't know you talked this way.'

'How?'

'Like us boys.'

'Not me. I don't talk like a boy. Boys are so stupid.'

I let it go.

Suddenly, covering her face with her hands, she laughed. 'I'm bad,' she said.

'Bad? I won't have you say that about yourself.'

'It's true. I'm a prankster.'

'Who isn't? Heh-heh! We all are, aren't we?'

'You're going to be mad with me, Beppo Tate.'

'Mad with you! Not in a thousand years!'

'Promise,' she said.

'Promise.'

'Your goat didn't really break the rope, you know.'

I smiled. 'I know,' I said.

Oops!

She wiped the grin off her face real fast. 'You knew?'

'Yep.'

'And you didn't let on?'

'Nope.'

'Why, Beppo Tate, why?'

I shrugged my shoulders.

'How'd you know?' she asked.

I told her.

'I ought to stop talking to you.' She was pouting. She turned a straight back on me.

Oh boy! Girls are funny people. I guess women are too. They don't like to be upstaged. They must always surprise.

'Was I wrong in not letting on?'

'No. Not really.'

'Well . . . ?'

'See you in school,' she said.

'Hey! What about the punishment for Teppy?' I said. 'Aren't we supposed to be fixing one for him? What do you think it should be?'

'Blackmail, of course,' she said with utmost coolness which, to me, hinged on cruelty. 'What else?'

'Blackmail?'

'It's fun,' she said.

'Fun? I don't think I know you, Daphne Belmont. Jeez! What can we ask for? Teppy's got no money. He doesn't even work.'

'Who wants money?' said Daphne. 'There are better things. Teppy's got the best mangoes in the village. They're called Reddies. Or don't you know? People come from all around to buy them. They're so good. Haven't you seen the tree in his yard?'

'I have, I have. Oh boy. How many per day? I'm getting to like this, Daphne. You're a genius.'

'Is twelve too steep?'

'Twelve it is. Six for me, six for you.'

'Picked and delivered here,' she said. 'We'll point out a place near here and he'll have to leave them there. Whether I see you or not you'll take your six and I'll take mine. How about that?'

'Great,' I said. 'Though I'd rather see you.'

Surprise. Whether feigned or genuine. But very well expressed.

'Whatever for?'

'A little chit-chat, maybe,' said I.

'We have enough chit-chat at school, Beppo Tate. I better go.'

The sun was rising, the rays licking the tree tops.

'Thanks for making me catch Teppy,' I said.

'It was nothing. 'Bye.'

'See you in school, Daphne.'

She was going but she turned. 'Do you like my name?'

'Oh, it's beautiful. Beautiful, beautiful.'

And then she was gone.

Nice girl. Strong personality. And my friend at last. Hallelujah!

CHAPTER 15

Matchmakers

The night of the school concert was the night of nights. Oh boy. It caused things to collapse and others to build.

So many people were there.

Everybody was dressed up, but I've always found dressed-up children smarter than dressed-up adults. Especially the girls, pacing around in frills and pony tails, buckled shoes and anklets.

The teachers too. Mr Ladd, the principal, was smarter than a new penny, wearing a new suit and a narrow tie with a flower in his lapel. In his hair was a path a half an inch wide. No less.

Our Miss Clemens was decked out in a dress with flouncy skirt but a gathered wasp-waist. Her hat didn't deserve to be called that at all because the blessed contraption – whatever it was – had one devil of a rim but lacked a crown. But she was swell and beaming, her black eyes glittering something beautiful.

Mr Ladd paused to chat with her. I hate to see a man twirl his fingers. Sign of shyness. But Mr Ladd was doing it. Maybe he poured compliments after compliments on her. She smiled ever so sweetly and since she had the best of teeth in the entire hall it was something to see. Genteel woman. Good teacher, too.

To see their children perform, sing, or recite, parents were there in droves. Pipe tobacco raided the sweet air.

Chatter and bursts of laughter filled it. The Old Man . . .
Mrs Belmont, although those two sat miles apart.

With a perpetual hissing sound the two gas lamps burned
at both ends of the hall.

A welcome to parents and opening remarks by the
principal.

Ladies and gen*til*men, boys and girls, etcetera, etcetera . . .
He was moving from flat feet to tip-toe.

Then the Master of Ceremonies, a Mr Livingstone, a big
farmer, paunchy as he was wealthy, took over. I was happy
that he wasn't supposed to give a long speech because for
every two words he spoke he cleaned his throat once.

Daphne, of course, was first on the stage.

A recitation.

No stage fright whatsoever. Hands clasped about waist-
high. Face clean and aglow. Voice bell-clear, enunciation
knife-sharp.

I wandered lonely as a cloud . . .

She was really cute: her eyes gas-lighted, her dress pink,
her shoes mirror bright and buckled.

Big ovation, whistles included.

A song by the choir.

Another ovation.

A second recitation, this time by George Kirby who, after
the first six lines was just like a stuck phonograph record.

'And . . .

And . . .

And . . .' until he blew his ruddy cool with a hiss of the
teeth and leapt – I repeat: leapt – from the stage.

But the audience was kind. They clapped and it wasn't
any different from the real ovation. Someone even said, 'He
tried.' And he had. How he had!

Then it was poor Roy up there. My little friend Roy
Penner. A perfect jug of a boy. Had bad stage manners

enough for six people. Throughout his performance he kept his hands deep in his pockets and his eyes on his toes. And a song from him! Something about a Bobby Shafto or other.

Frankly, I had heard him practise and he had done quite well but, apparently, there is no reckoning of the damage that stage fright can do to a person. Because it was the worst singing I had ever heard delivered either in private or in public. At the end I had a mind to stand up and say: 'Those were the words, Roy, what about letting us have the tune now?' but I left it unsaid and our considerate audience gave him the insides of their hands.

I'm not bragging when I say that Daphne and I, in our play, stole the show. Not the entire concert show: just the play. Our acting was good. Of course other things helped. For atmosphere we had some kind of a set and Daphne had brought a great pot to be her witch's cauldron and we were dressed for our parts, she in a black hat with a deep pointed crown, and so on, and I equipped with pitchfork and wearing work clothes.

The story in capsule.

The prince on hearing of the beauty of the princess, journeys many miles to the court of the king and queen to ask for the princess's hand. On his way, there is a storm and, on seeing a light, he seeks shelter. But it is a witch who lives there, a toothy hag who, on seeing the handsome devil of a prince, swoons witch swoons and swears she will marry him.

Naturally, he finds her repulsive and rejects her.

Naturally she aims to get him by hook or crook and when he is asleep she prepares a brew in a great cauldron and proceeds to feed him some. But as she wakes him and would do her evil, in rushes a farmer (me), forbidding the prince to drink.

Well, there's a righteous good squabble between witch

and farmer. The latter saves the prince from the débâcle and is handsomely rewarded as a future royal guard. But on to the king's court they journey, where the witch is put on trial, the farmer once more giving evidence.

Of course my acting was further helped by the handsome but dumb prince who filled the stage with:

I don't believe it, Is this true about yonder lady? A witch? Woe is me. Canst thou prove it?

And I:

Sir, prince, it's not only true. But I will prove it.

Daphne:

'Tis not true, handsome prince. My lord, my liege, my everything.

I:

Shut up, you miserable woman.

Playing opposite Daphne helped immensely, too. Even in real life she was quite a perky devil and the sort to bring a boy's blood to the boil. All the time I thought it to be real. I wanted to grab and shake the witchery out of her. I pointed, stood akimbo, knelt before dumb-dumb prince and jumped up just as fast and as airy as someone with wings – if there is such a thing – and when we were through, with Daphne weeping genuine witch tears, that audience roared and jumped to their feet and banged the floor. And it went on for fully five minutes.

The cast came out and we took a bow. The king: Mark Dunn; the queen: sulky and fat Marcia Donaldson; dumb-dumb prince: Tony Carr; the princess: Leona Perez; Daphne and I.

All in all we had a whopping concert and the MC made the usual remarks about 'the unparalleled excellence' of the concert and referred to the fact that we were 'second to none'.

Then Mr Ladd, on tip-toe of course, thanked everybody,

pouring it especially on Miss Clemens who had done 'so much, so much, much' to make it a success.

Then we sang the anthem, everybody, and our rendition of it could have drawn as many laughs as Roy's *Bobby Shafto*. After that everybody mingled freely, commenting, shaking hands, waiting for their children, praising them. Some began to leave the hall.

And now for the best part of the night.

The Old Man wished to congratulate me and Mrs Belmont wanted to praise Daphne and we, the actors, were standing together talking. Consider the implications.

'You were fine, Beppo,' he said.

'Daphne, you were a gem,' she said.

They bumped into each other.

'Oh, pardon me, Mrs Belmont.'

'It's all right,' she said with one of those puffed-jawed smiles, even turning to glance at Dad.

His mouth fell open and remained open for a second or two. Poor love-stricken man.

'You, young man,' she said to me. 'You were excellent, too.'

'Thank you, ma'am.'

The Old Man said, 'Aren't they something? The young people of today – you can't stop them! Accept my congratulations, Daphne.'

'Say, thank you, Daphne,' said her mother.

'Thanks,' she said, late only because she, like myself, was surprised at seeing the two arch-enemies breaking up the ice.

'It was a very good concert,' said the Old Man.

'Very enriching,' said Mrs Belmont. 'We should have something like this more often. Cultural enrichment.'

'And so we should.'

I had Daphne aside. 'My God,' I said. 'Look what the concert's done!'

'They're talking again,' she said. 'And it's for real.'

'I'm so glad,' I said.

'Me too,' she said.

'Why are you glad?' I asked.

'Silly boy,' she said.

We laughed.

'You think it's the concert alone?' I asked.

'What do you mean, Beppo Tate?'

'I mean, do you think there is something else that caused it? Some little thing? Or people?'

She looked deep into my eyes and laughed.

'You,' she said. 'You're something else.'

Again we laughed.

'I'll get my cauldron,' she said.

'Oh no, you don't. It's too heavy for a girl.'

'Big joke. I carried it here.'

'Because I wasn't there to help. Can't you see? But now, I'll take it.'

'It's very nice of you,' Daphne said with gas-lighted teeth. Her eyes danced like a fairy's.

'Let's go, you two,' the Old Man said.

More than three-quarters of the crowd had left already.

Daphne and I went on the stage to get the pot – oops, cauldron – and when we returned we found that the Old Man and Mrs Belmont were still busy breaking up ice patches with conversation and smiles and the use of first and surnames, and I felt warm and confident and double-glad.

When we reached Mrs Belmont's gate the Old Man said, 'Goodnight, Martha. It was very nice seeing you tonight and our little talk was delightful.'

'It's the same here, Tate.'

'Goodnight.'

Before she could say anything I said: 'But, Dad, I have to carry this cauldron up to the house for Daphne.'

He looked down. 'Oh, I see you're a lady's gentleman.'

'Isn't he cute?' said Mrs Belmont, and she meant it. I knew it.

'Well, I can't see how I can interfere with gentlemanly conduct, can I?'

'Not at all,' said Mrs Belmont.

And so we went on across the yard.

'Nice night, Martha,' he said.

'Be-autiful!' she said.

Actually there was nothing nice about it, not with the inky darkness and the few stars just barely able to peep through, not with the rags of cloud scudding along overhead. Except they referred to the hundreds of fireflies snaking their light in the blackness which was something *I* liked.

'Would you like to come in for a coffee, Tate?'

'Yes, ma'am,' I said.

'Since when's your name Tate?' the Old Man asked without irritation.

Daphne and I laughed. We were doing so many things – conspiring, acting, speaking, laughing.

We went into the house, Mrs Belmont leading the way, Daphne next, the Old Man and I manfully manning the rear.

Glorious night.

Coffee, pudding, milk and talk.

Wonderful.

CHAPTER 16

Mangoes, mangoes

Of course I had communicated to Teppy the terms under which he must suffer blackmail: twelve juicy mangoes to be delivered daily at a certain spot. And each day he came through with a nest egg of mangoes of the pinkest cheeks.

Those mangoes were of first-class quality. Reddies. When you deprived them of their skins and put them into your mouth they just melted. Well, you couldn't put one in all at once, any one of them being too large for that, but you put it in one section at a time and it melted section by section. And what was more: they were sweeter than sweet.

With utmost delight and mischief, Daphne and I enjoyed them day after day. Sometimes we met and had joint repasts of mangoes. Or just had a tête-à-tête. Or maybe joked at Teppy's expense.

'Isn't this something, getting these mangoes free,' she'd say.

'Thanks to you, Daphne. It was a brilliant idea. That Teppy! Serves him right though. He's double mad.'

'Is he?'

'Doesn't even come around the house any more.'

'Good. He's just a parasite anyway.'

'Did I tell you about the owl I fed him?'

'What? You don't say.'

'Oh yes.'

I told her the details.

She laughed giggles, then splutters, finally tears.

'Ahoo! Patoo!' I said.

'You're a devil, Beppo.'

'Thank you, dear.'

Snappy seriousness. 'Don't you dear me.'

That Daphne. Hard as nails. But I liked girls that way.

One afternoon, for old time's sake and because I had nothing better to do, I wandered up to Teppy's home. From a distance I could see the mango tree, now at its high point in mango production. There were so many pink and crimson ones throughout the foliage. And what was that? Sounded like a dog barking. Had Teppy acquired a dog?

I advanced with utmost care and found that there was indeed a dog, but thankfully on a rope, the rope being anchored on to the mango tree. Teppy meant business all right. He certainly wasn't taking any chances with boy prowlers. His mangoes were really pink gold to him. A dog to guard them.

Two adults who had bought two basketsful of fruits were on the point of leaving. At three pence a dozen he was reeling in money.

Teppy was very gracious with his customers, asking them to come again. Anytime. There would be mangoes for them, he promised.

Because I had taken care to conceal myself behind a banana tree, neither dog nor owner had detected my presence. The dog was as huge as a moderate-sized goat but scrawny as ever. If I had the mind to I would have been able to count his ribs without really trying hard. I didn't know its disposition because it was quiet now. But as soon as I stepped into the open and cleaned my throat, both wheeled on me and the dog lurched and strained on his rope, barking like the devil, raging to get at me.

'You . . . you criminal!' Teppy screamed at me, trying so hard to outdo the dog. 'What you doin' in me yard? I 'ave a min' lettin' this bloodhoun' loose on you, you blackmailer an' cheat. You an' your ladyfrien', you rob me out o' twelve mangoes a day. Three pence a day! Lord, boy, I tell you, you's criminal in every bone an' thru an' thru. You's the devil in hell. Look what you done to Tate an' me! I don' even see 'im any more . . .'

'I didn't tell you to steal his milk and feel guilty about it, Teppy.'

'Don' give me any lip, boy. You done ruin a good frien'-ship. You went an' got 'im sweet on that Mrs Beltshazzar an' now 'e's got eyes only for 'er. Don' deny it 'cause I know you done it. You got sweet on Daphne an' led Tate to get sweet on the modher. You? You don' stan' a chance wit' me, boy. The firs' look I got o' you that Sunday mornin' I knew you 'ad bad blood . . .'

The dog shifted into low gear, growling in his throat.

' . . . The moment you make a wrong move, boy, I mean to skin you. Make fun of a big respect'ble man like me! Feed me owl meat then turn roun', as dry eye as ever, an' blackmail me! "Twelve mangoes, Teppy. Six for me an' six for me sweet'eart." (Of course I hadn't used the word 'sweetheart'.) 'You' sweet'eart, huh! Well, I got news for you, blackmailer. This mango season don' las' forever an' when it's done I goin' to wash me hands o' you . . .'

'Who says?'

'Who says? You see this dog? You know what make 'e is? 'E's got bloodhoun' qualities, boy. 'E'll make mince-meat o' you. If you ever as much as wander in me yard when I'm not aroun' 'e'll snap off your devil's head an' the world will be rid of a scoundrel . . .'

'Hah!'

'Hah as many hahs as you please, boy, but 'ear this. I

feed 'im special for you. I feed 'im wasp nest an' raw meat . . .'

I tittered. 'Owl meat?'

He made a step or two towards me and the dog, interpreting this as a cue to launch another offensive, lurched and leaped and barked at me.

'You see, boy?' said Teppy. 'Take care. This dog's been programmed for you' t'roat. Take a good look at 'em mangoes but cut your eyes. Get no fancy ideas to come 'ere wit' your stealin' self. Or else . . .' He grinned. 'Boy, do I 'ave news for you! I's goin' out t'morrow, all day, an' don' get no ideas 'bout settin' foot up 'ere as you jus' done now. 'Cause this 'ere dog's no respecter o' boys' flesh. Keep away I tell you 'cause this dog'll be chained right 'ere all day guardin' 'is master's int'rest. Now get out o' me sight before I let 'im rip.'

'Ahoo!' I said. 'Patoo!'

'Get, you . . . !'

My 'ahoo' and 'patoo' upset the dog who began to bark even more furiously than before, leaping in the rope. He had an old dog's eyes, and *was* old, but his mouth was massive and his fangs vicious. He probably could burst his leash. I left.

All that was a lot of words to make me afraid. Teppy couldn't have meant all that had passed through his mouth. His was an attempt to make me respect his Methuselah of a dog and fear him. He was severely put out by my trapping him and collecting twelve mangoes per day.

I went away, pondering the situation.

Tomorrow he'd be absent. Mangoes were on the tree in great pink numbers. His dog would be standing guard. Don't set foot in that yard. It was so much like an invitation.

On the following day I discussed the problem with Roy. He heard me out to the very end then he said:

'That's bad, old man. We must do something about that dog. He's been brainwashed to hate you and we have to un-brainwash him.'

'Un-brainwash him?'

'You're too particular about grammar, old man.'

'But do it how?'

'Leave that to me. You said Teppy'll be away all day tomorrow?'

'That's what he said.'

'Goody. After school we'll pay his dog a visit, old man.'

'If you say so, Roy.'

After school we met on the track by the river, which is between my house and Teppy's. Roy was carrying a two-gallon basket made of bamboo.

'What's the basket for?' I asked.

'Mangoes.'

'But . . .'

'Old man,' he said like a philosopher or breadwinner or something. 'If we have to make the trip up there we might as well have some mangoes while we're there.'

All this, of course, made good sense, but I wouldn't have thought of it. This boy never ceased to amaze me.

We walked towards Teppy's and I was pondering the workings of Roy's mind. He was so cool, so melancholy, so soft, so severely angelic but so danged cunning.

'You're a genius,' I told him.

'Why?'

'Well . . . you think up the most marvellous and amazing things.'

'Oh, it's nothing.'

Oh, it's nothing, oh, it's nothing.

I was so impressed with all this that we were clear up to the edge of Teppy's yard before I remembered to ask Roy what he meant to do about the dog which was lying under the mango tree, leashed as his master had promised, dozing with his ugly long muzzle resting on his forepaws.

Calmly Roy dug in his pocket and surfaced with a large fire-cracker.

'A left-over from last Christmas,' he said.

His voice carried to the dog which awoke with a rocketing upwards of its head and a sharp bark. When he saw us he went wild all right, jumping up, barking, leaping towards us. But each time the rope jerked him back and I thought he might even break his neck and save Roy the trouble.

Roy's activity soon grabbed my attention away from the dog. Calmly, he was getting a match ready and I understood that he meant to use some artillery.

'We stand close together,' he said, 'so that the dog'll see that what scares him comes from us both.'

We stood close.

He lit the match and touched it to the fuse of the fire-cracker then tossed it curving towards doggie. It burst in mid-air but that was enough. He switched directions faster than the eye could monitor and leapt a great curve like an earnest deer and even before he landed again the rope leash snapped. And that dog went like a bullet. When he rounded the corner of the house his spine made a perfect right-angle with it and while we laughed we could still hear the gaffer cutting a mighty swath through bushes and scrubs, over dell and vale too. I was positive that full twenty minutes after we left the premises, that that dog was still running.

I laughed my head off.

But Roy didn't waste time on the humour of the situation for he was a more practical thief than that. Instead he shinnied up into the tree, jumping, nimbly like a monkey, from branch to branch, giving each the identical treatment: a thorough shaking. Mangoes rained down – *Bif! Bif! Bif!*

and *Bif!* again. I ran around, filling Roy's basket and my pocket.

Then he was down in a flash and we were on our way. At a safe distance we stopped and enjoyed the situation as well as some mangoes.

'Roy,' I said. 'You're magnificent.'

'Oh, it was nothing.'

'That dog really went,' I said.

'He won't bother you nor me from now on,' he said. 'When he sees us he's going to wish he was someplace else.'

'You're a genius,' I said. 'What would you like to be when you grow up?' I asked.

'Nothing,' he replied, busy eating a mango.

'Nothing! With a brain like yours?' I bit into a new mango. 'You ought to be a scientist,' I said.

'What's a scientist?'

'A man of course.'

He suffered me a rebuking look. 'I know that. What does he do?'

'Oh, invents things. Machines. Makes rockets and things like cars.'

'Oh boy, I love cars,' he said brightening. 'You know what, old man, the first thing I'm going to buy when I start making money's a car.'

'With a brain like yours you won't have to buy one, Roy. You'll be able to make your own.'

'You're crazy,' he said.

We ate some more mangoes then went home.

CHAPTER 17

Two plus two equals zero

In a matter of weeks everything had happened. The Old Man was paying Mrs Belmont regular evening visits, taking me along and, once, too, we were invited to Sunday dinner. It wasn't long before he broke the news to me that he would be marrying Martha. I expressed great delight because I thought that it was going to be a handsome package indeed, he and his Martha, and me and my Daphne. I really liked that girl.

The wedding was about a month off when I cornered Daphne for some chit-chat.

'Are you going to be a flower girl?' I asked.

'Of course not! It's not going to be that kind of wedding,' she said.

'What do you mean, Daphne – not that kind of wedding?'

'My mom's been married before you know!'

'I know that.'

'She's a widow.'

'So?'

'If you allow me I'll tell you, you know, Beppo Tate.'

Here came the crispy-missy style again.

'If a woman's been married before, she doesn't wear a veil and gown at her second or third wedding. She wears a short dress and there's not much of the usual trappings.'

'Trappings or not I'm going to be a page boy,' I said.

'No, you're not.'

'Who says?'

'If there's no flower girl, there's no page boy, stupid.'

'Well, what kind of wedding's that?'

'I've told you. I just told you.'

She stood up from the log where we were seated and, holding her hem with both hands, preened around and around like a prairie chicken.

I was deeply disappointed by this injection of new information into the business of weddings. I couldn't see why people had to observe stupid rules and not have a proper wedding. I hoped, at least, that they would kill a goat and curry it and have cakes and drinks to wash the entire mess down.

'Do you think you'll get married when you grow up, Daphne?' I asked, coming out of the mini-gloom.

'Of course I will.'

'Whom to?'

'How'd I know, boob?'

'But you must have a little bitty idea of him.'

'Well . . .' and she mocked up the fellow in her mind, taking time to ponder him.

'. . . he'll be tall . . .'

I could fit the bill, yes I could. I had the earmarks of tallness in my bones.

'. . . and he'll be dark . . .'

My exact colour.

'. . . . and handsome . . .'

Nothing to worry about there. Better than a dozen times I had been told I was handsome, by george. All of me was there in what she sought.

'. . . And of course,' she added, 'I'll look for other little things . . .'

'What other little things?'

'I'll make sure,' said she, 'that he's clean in his ways and has a nice-sounding name. I like nice names.'

I saw what she was getting at.

'Beppo's not my last name, you know,' I said. 'So you needn't worry that you'll be called Daphne Beppo.'

'Beppo!' Her eyes came out of her head all right. 'What are you talking about? You think I would marry you?'

Deflation.

'You wouldn't? Why not?'

She laughed. 'Silly boy. Little girls don't grow up marrying their brothers.'

'I'm not your brother,' I jumped to my feet and said.

'You will be.'

'Me? Your brother? You got to be joking.'

'You'll be calling my mom Ma or Mom; and I'll be saying Pa or Dad to Mr Tate.'

'Good grief!' She had a point.

'But still I won't be your sister.'

'Of course not,' she laughed. 'You won't be my sister . . . My brother.'

'You know what I mean. This is stupid,' I said, stamping my foot.

'Facts of life,' she said.

'Son of a gun,' I said.

Then she was gone, skipping lightly and singing: *Here Comes the Bride*. I could have killed that girl. That know-all.

Stupid woman that Martha, I said.

The bad thing was Daphne was acting as though she was happy that we weren't going to marry – and with all the work I had put in. Son of a gun.

I cheered up only when Roy joined me. He noted that I was down in the mouth and said, 'How about a smoke, old man?'

'Good,' I said. 'Just what I need.'

We each rolled a paper cigarette and walked away to a more secluded spot and lit up.

'You know, Roy,' I said. 'I've been keeping an eye on Marcia of late. She's not a bad-looking girl, you know.'

'Which Marcia?' he asked with some speed.

'Marcia Donaldson. You know the one.'

'Not bad-looking you say?'

'She's beautiful, Roy.'

He settled back. He said, 'If you look long and hard, I guess she's okay.'

'What the heck do you mean?'

'Well, if you look quickly, she's – yech!'

Imagine him, the rat-like scamp, saying such unworthies about a perfectly beautiful girl. Ah well . . .

Marcia was the sulky loner in our class. The champion candy eater. A bit on the fat side.

'I like girls like Marcia,' I told Roy. 'Girls who are pretty-faced aren't the best, Roy. Listen to an experienced man. It's the other one who's beautiful. The one who's a plain Jane on the outside. Like Marcia. Know what I mean?'

Roy didn't know what I meant.

'What about Daphne?' he asked.

'Oh, she! She's too pretty, Roy. She's the kind I'm talking of, man. She's not really beautiful 'cause there's nothing beneath . . . like qualities. She can't be kind; she's cruel. Can't be sweet but miserable. She's boastful, she's bossy and everything. She's the kind who'll run around too . . .'

He watched me in shocked silence, pulling puff after puff of smoke down as though his very life depended on it.

'We wouldn't make the ideal couple. We wouldn't get along. Already that girl's getting on my nerves,' I said. 'She's even stealing Dad away from me. She comes over in the afternoons, grinning like a Cheshire cat and shows Dad her books. Her arithmetic. Her stupid compositions. "Look, Mr Tate," she says. "See, all my sums are right. And I got 90 for this composition." So he looks at me, the Old Man does. "And you, Beppo? Where's your book?" I get my book and there are two sums right and two wrong. And as for the wretched composition I have a fifty-five. See what I mean? She's thoroughly mean. Soon, when that fool wedding takes place, she'll be the darling and I'll be plain nothing.'

'H'mm,' Roy said. And that was all he said.

'I think Marcia's better.'

'You're crazy, old man,' Roy said. 'Marcia's impossible.'

'Exactly,' I said. 'I've broken down Daphne and I'm now looking for newer challenges, man.' I choked on a puff and coughed. 'The tougher a girl is the more fun to break her down and make her eat out of your hands. Take Daphne. When I got here that girl really hated me inside out and you saw what I did to her within a week or two. I made her talk to me and even become my bosom friend and accomplice too. See what I mean? But already I feel tired of her, Roy. No joking. I'm going to go after Marcia. She's a loner and always aloof and I like the challenge.'

'Good luck, old man. If she grows up as fat as she is, she's going to cost you a lot for clothes.'

'What's an extra couple of yards?'

'And in food too. I bet that girl eats like a horse,' Roy said.

'So I'll be able to feed her. You think I'm going to be a pauper or something?'

'Good luck just the same.'

'What, you don't seem to agree!'

'I'm confused,' he said. 'I thought you really liked Daphne.'

'I do, but don't you see? She'll be my sister soon!'

'So that's it!' said Roy, lighting up in the face and arms and legs. 'That's it!'

'Isn't that a shame?' I said, confessing. 'And all the work I put in! Now, very soon, we'll be living like sister and brother.'

'I'm sorry, old man.'

'Two plus two equals zero,' I said from somewhat far away.

'What?' he asked, laughing. 'Two plus two equals four!' He had another laugh. 'One day in class you said two plus two equalled blackmail. Now two plus two equals zero.'

'Exactly,' I said. 'We're two. The Old Man and I. And they're two. Daphne and her stupid mother. But soon, after that wedding, we'll be one and for me that's zero. I'll have nothing.'

'Jeez!' Roy said. 'I see what you mean. That's real smart, old man. Boy, I really like you. I really like how you put things.'

'Thanks, Roy. But I know what I'll do. I'll bust the stupid marriage up. If I hadn't shoved my stupid face around her there wouldn't be no stupid marriage and I'll bust it up. Clean, clean, clean. There'll be a divorce. You watch.'

'You will bust up the marriage?'

'Watch.'

'You must like Daphne a lot, old man.'

'Of course. All the way. She's a beaut.'

'Two plus two equals zero,' he mused.

'I'm going home,' I said. I got up. I felt rotten.

'See you around, old man,' Roy said. I bet he took it just as hard as I.

'Boy,' he said as I was walking away. 'Two plus two equals zero. And he's right.'

I went home.

The Author

Everard Palmer was born in Jamaica and lived there until a few years ago. His childhood was spent in a village not unlike the village of this story.

He now lives in Canada and divides his time between writing and teaching.

He has had a number of stories published and also available in this series is *The Hummingbird People*

Authors of the Caribbean is a series of short stories and novels. The authors include Michael Anthony, Monica Skeete and Everard Palmer.

Nelsons also publish:

New West Indian Readers Infant Storybooks for primary school children:
Spot and Tippy
Looking after Tim
A Day on the Farm
A Day at the Sea

Tamarind Books for secondary school children:

The Shark Hunters	Andrew Salkey
A Drink of Water	Samuel Selvon
Monkey Liver Soup	Eaulin Ashtine
King of the Masquerade	Michael Anthony
The Upturned Turtles	Lilla Stirling
The Iguana's Tail	Sir Philip Sherlock

Biographies of famous West Indian cricketers:
Sir Learie Constantine
Sir Frank Worrell
Sir Garfield Sobers
George Headley